101

TRAINING
ACTIVITIES
& How To Run Them

Written by Derek Good and Craig McFadyen

Contents

Dedication

We would like to dedicate this book to all the people who have been on any of our training courses and have been subjected to these activities and ideas!

We thank you for being part of the group of people who helped us become better facilitators by learning from you as we watched you progress through our courses.

Keep on learning.

About the authors

The authors have over 30 years joint experience and have been designing and running training, coaching and leadership sessions for companies of all sizes and government departments in multiple countries.

The activities in this book have been put together based on actual used and proven activities that will give you great results for your teams and training sessions.

The activities have been structured in such a way that they are easy to find to suit your particular need, each activity is set out the same way to ensure consistency and ease of use and application.

Once you are familiar with these activities you can begin experimenting with them in different ways and morphing them to suit your needs.

Some suggested areas you can use these activities for could be:

- Induction programmes

- Team meetings

- Coaching sessions

- Training sessions

- Team building

- Motivational sessions

- Improve communication

- Just having fun!

We hope you enjoy these activities as much as we did.

Introduction

Why Use Activities? Since learning involves participants interacting with one another, it makes sense that they should also learn in situations presented by activities. There are additional reasons why an interactive experiential approach results in effective learning such as these:

Cognitive Science Research. Studies indicate that people learn more effectively and apply their newly learned knowledge and skills more easily through activities. Research on such diverse areas like stress, anxiety, creativity, and self-efficacy reinforce the generalization that we need to play more in order to improve our learning.

Multiple Intelligences. Recent studies on the nature of intelligence have eliminated traditional IQ measures as the sole indicator of effective performance. Newer frame-works of intelligence emphasize that there are several avenues to learning other than the conventional use of language and logic. Games and activities tap into alternative intelligences.

Adult Learning Theory. Most adults bring a rich store of experiences to the learning situation. The primary task of the facilitator is to help them, through collaborative efforts, to derive generalizations from this base of experience.

Emotional Learning. Events that are accompanied by emotions result in long-lasting learning. ***Boredom is not conducive to effective learning***. Activities that include appropriate levels of cooperation within teams and competition across teams add emotional elements to learning.

Practice and Feedback. Learners cannot master skills without repeated practice and feedback. Activities provide opportunities for practicing interpersonal skills and for receiving immediate feedback from peers.

Why Use Activities During Training

Activities are a great tool for enhancing learning, getting people to relax and introduce themselves but can also be used in a wide variety of uses outside the training room as well, such as getting communication moving during team meetings and energizing your teams if you feel they need a boost during the day.

If being used in a classroom environment, activities are a great way to break up long periods of PowerPoint or talking and can help keep the group focussed, energy levels high through movement while reinforcing key messages you are sending through interactivity.

Some psychologists claim the typical student's attention span is **about 10 to 15 minutes** long, yet most university classes last **50 to 90 minutes**. It's natural for student attention levels to vary according to motivation, mood, perceived relevance of the material, and other factors.

CONE OF LEARNING   (EDGAR DALE)

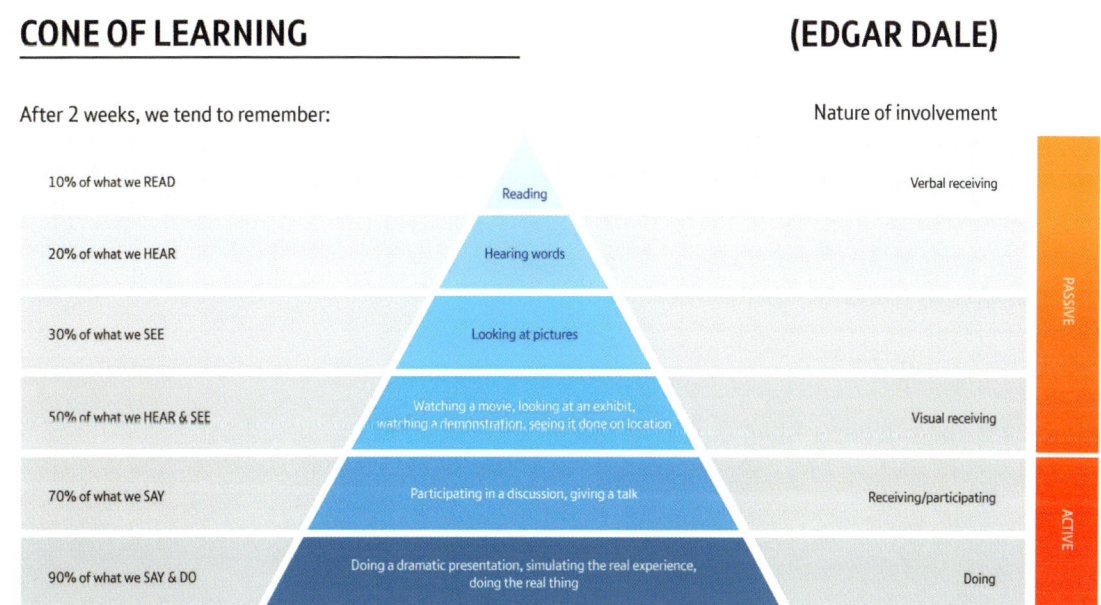

After 2 weeks, we tend to remember:

Nature of involvement

10% of what we READ	Reading	Verbal receiving
20% of what we HEAR	Hearing words	
30% of what we SEE	Looking at pictures	
50% of what we HEAR & SEE	Watching a movie, looking at an exhibit, watching a demonstration, seeing it done on location	Visual receiving
70% of what we SAY	Participating in a discussion, giving a talk	Receiving/participating
90% of what we SAY & DO	Doing a dramatic presentation, simulating the real experience, doing the real thing	Doing

PASSIVE

ACTIVE

Therefore it is vital that we use activities to drive home our key points at the correct time:

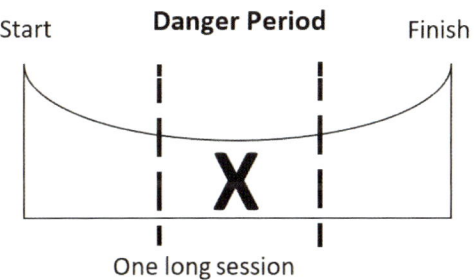

Start   **Danger Period**   Finish

X

One long session

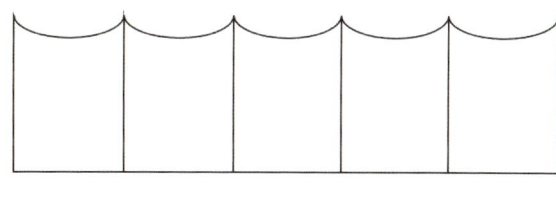

Short sessions with opening and closing

A session with regular breaks or movement

There are four key things to remember to implement a successful activity:

- You must know what outcome you are going to achieve by using it

- You must know how to run the activity and have practiced it well beforehand

- You must know how to debrief the activity for it to make sense and formulate a link

- You must know how to show the direct link between learning outcome and the training being covered for the group to get the Ah Ha! moment.

Make sure when training that you refer to activities as activities and not games, games are for parties and children (which is fine if you are teaching children and not adults) as there is a difference in thinking from how adults will be asked to play games when they are in a training session. However, frame your statement as 'Right lets run an activity to show you…'

Trainers, coaches and leaders need to use a range of different activities depending what message or state change is wanting to be achieved; are you reinforcing a key point or wanting people to open up and talk? Different use of different activities will generate different outcomes

Different types of activities include:

- Icebreakers
- Energisers
- Role plays

- Motivators
- State Changes

One thing to make sure of is that the activity is shown how its outcomes directly relate back to the learning.

If using activities in a classroom you need to ensure that when the activity is finished people understand the clear link and learning that has occurred. If you simply run an activity then move on, the group will lose their learning as they will be hung up on *why did we do that?* Similarly, if you run too many activities the group will become fatigued and learning will be lost so there is a fine line to choosing and running your activities to get maximum results.

Tips on using activities:

☑ Know the connection & result you want the group to reach

☑ Know how to run the activity clearly and smoothly

☑ Use your activities at the right time for the right reasons

☑ Plan your activities before your training not on the fly

☑ Have more activities than you need for your training

The Importance of Objectives & Activities

By planning your training outline prior to your training session (this too includes meetings and coaching sessions) you will be able to see quite clearly where the best place will be for using an activity or energizer to boost the group and reinforce a key point or outcome of the training.

This planning and linking to the learning outcomes is what will make your session far more enjoyable and flow a lot more smoothly than jumping around trying to drop in activities or energizers for the sake of it.

If you have a particularly heavy or boring topic then the correct use and timing of activities during the session will have a greater impact on the learning and energy levels of your group.

Giving Activity Instructions

One of the most overlooked and assumed skills in a trainer's toolkit is the ability to control a group and maintain a sense of everything being the groups idea. This control needs to start at the outset of the training session with the trainer being confident, assertive and consistent.

When giving instructions it is vital that you are consistent on how you deliver the steps of the activity to ensure the group will follow you. If you are unsure the group will pick up on this and may impact on your credibility and their learning.

Time and time again we have witnessed trainers getting frustrated with their groups because they have lost control during an activity and had to repeat themselves over and over again (to the point where one trainer has been witnessed shouting at their group!) so the frustration of the trainer damages the relationship with the group and they will be less likely to want to engage in future activities.

Follow this simple technique for giving instructions and if done consistently and assertively watch how quickly your groups will follow your lead:

Simple Instructions

When giving instructions we have to have complete control of the group. This is a habit that is very easy to develop with the group providing you are consistent with your instructions. Before you know it they will be following your instructions to the letter!

When giving instructions to a group remember these points:

- Know exactly what you want them to do
- Keep it short and concise
- Confirm clarification before beginning
- Ensure control of the group by being assertive
- Give time frames

Here are six easy steps for giving activity instructions:

- Get Attention from the group
- When I say go… (Load the gun) emphasize the GO
- What I want you to do is….(Give instructions) (Aim the gun)
- Any questions on that? (Seek clarification)
- You'll have about 5 minutes for this (Timeframes)
- OK then GO (Sound) (FIRE the gun) Make a sound such as a clap when you say GO

If you are consistent with this approach you will find that people won't move until you clap.

Instruction Tips

If the instructions are long or complicated then break them in chunks and have the group complete the instructions one chunk at a time before giving them the next one.

> **For example:**
>
> When I say **go** I want you split into pairs and spread out round the room then I'll give you your next set of instructions – go!
>
> When I say go I want you in your pairs to discuss the last topic and write the answers on a pad. Any questions on that?
>
> I'll give you about 5 minutes, OK **then Go!**

During The Activity

Ensure that you pay attention to the group while running an activity; running an activity is not an excuse for you to wander off and do something else leaving the group busy!   Walk around and observe the group and watch the interactions, identify any frustrations or confusion and step in to avoid any damage being done by them not understanding what to do.

By staying involved with the group while they are undertaking an activity shows you care about what happens and that you are not just using the activity to distract the group while you do something else or kill time.

Debrief After An Activity

It is vital that after running an activity you debrief the learnings that have occurred and link them to the topic being discussed. This will assist with reinforcing the learning and creating a memorable anchor for future retention and recall.

If you do not debrief after running an activity you may in fact hinder the learning you have been trying to achieve because the group may be confused as to why they completed the activity. Debriefing also helps the group express and discuss any internal feelings, outcomes or break throughs they may have experienced during the activity.

Failure to debrief an activity also can make it look like you are killing time or trying to 'pad out' your session. It's a fine balance between too few activities and losing the groups concentration and running too many activities and them appearing to be used for the wrong reasons.

If you always keep a few activities up your sleeve you can use them should your group speed through something faster than normal or you may need to swap out some text training for an activity to get a point across.

The important rule here is flexibility.

Defining The Activity Categories

To assist you with choosing the correct activity to suit your needs we have a quick explanation of each:

Icebreakers

An icebreaker is an activity to help people in a group start the process of getting to know each other. Ideally used with new groups who may not know each other or returning groups to reconnect with each other. Some ways they can be used might be at the start of an induction or training program or team meeting.

Energizers

An energizer is an activity that is run whenever the group is lagging or needs a boost. Using energizers helps break up the training and aids concentration of the group. Its also an opportunity to prepare a group prior to starting work or engaging with customers such as in a team meeting or team huddle.

Training Activities

Training activities are used to drive home a learning point while increasing concentration by introducing a change or something different from the current learning style. A training activity should always have a point for it being run and also a debrief that links it back to the training being covered.

Training Review Activities

Training review activities are vital to help reinforce the learning covered. The old adage of Tell them what you are going to tell them, tell them then tell them what you just told them helps increase memory and reinforcement through multiple coverage of the learning in different formats. This is also a great way to end the training on a fun note or starting a new day with a review of the learning from the previous day or session.

Activities List

ICEBREAKERS

ENERGISERS

ACTIVITIES

ACTIVITIES

ACTIVITIES

TRAINING REVIEW ACTIVITIES

STORIES

ICEBREAKERS

3 UNCOMMON THINGS

OBJECTIVE:

To help groups think outside the square and work together.

This helps people to be inclusive and contribute to a small group

MATERIAL REQUIRED:	TIME REQUIRED:
None	10 minutes

INSTRUCTIONS:

Divide the group into 3s and ask the small groups to come up with 3 things that they have in common. They must look for things which aren't obvious like hair colour, sex, age or nationality. Tell them they must come up with 3 things which are uncommon but common to them.

Have them share back with the wider group.

DE-BRIEF AND REVIEW:

ASK THEM:

- How did you get started?
- What made it easier to identify common things?
- What communication skills were needed most?

ACRONYM NAMES

OBJECTIVE:

To help a group get to know each other quickly. Great to use for a conference. Works great for those on tables to get to know each other.

MATERIAL REQUIRED:	TIME REQUIRED:
None	10 -15 minutes

INSTRUCTIONS:

Explain that we are going to do a quick exercise to get to know each other on our tables. This is called Acronym names. I'll show you how it is done. We're going to write our first name in letters down one side of a page and we are going to assign a word that says something about us or that we're interested in for each letter of our first name.

As an example, if my first name was DAVID, this is how it might look:

> D – Director (I am the director of my company)
>
> A – Apples (I love apples and try to eat at least one per day)
>
> V – Very in to comedy (I love comedy and watch comedy shows whenever I can).
>
> I – Iceland (I went to Iceland last year on holiday – it was amazing!)
>
> D – Department Store (I love shopping and especially department store shopping)

Make sure the group knows what's going to happen and tell them to start. Give them a few minutes to come up with something for each letter. Tell them they can be creative – like V can be 'Very happy'. If they have multiple letters in their name – they need to come up with something different for each letter regardless.

If someone has a long name and they are struggling, allow them to shorten it – like William to Will or Samantha to Sam.

Offer your help to people that are obviously struggling. Walk around and encourage. When you think most people are done, get them to share their information with the rest of the table.

DE-BRIEF AND REVIEW:

ASK THEM

- Who learned something new?
- Who would like to share something amazing?

BANK ON IT

OBJECTIVE:

This icebreaker helps to start a training session off on a positive note. It is useful to highlight how we all benefit from positive feedback and challenges participants to consider how often they provide it themselves.

The icebreaker is particularly useful in training sessions such as; Great Leadership Skills, Assertiveness Skills, Building Relationships, Emotional Intelligence and Leading Effective Teams.

MATERIAL REQUIRED:	TIME REQUIRED:
None	10 – 15 minutes

INSTRUCTIONS:

Explain the concept of the 'Emotional Bank Account' as follows…

We all know what a financial bank account is. We make deposits into it and build up a reserve from which we can make withdrawals when we need to. An Emotional Bank Account is a metaphor that describes the amount of trust that's been built up in a relationship. It's the feeling of safeness you have with another human being.

If I make deposits into an Emotional Bank Account with you through courtesy, kindness, honesty, and keeping my commitments to you, I build up a reserve. Your trust toward me becomes higher, and I can call upon that trust many times if I need to. I can even make mistakes and that trust level will compensate for it.

When you are sure that participants understand the concept of the emotional bank account, ask them to introduce themselves to the rest of the group by stating their name and providing two examples from this working week that demonstrate how they have paid into the 'emotional bank account' they have with another person i.e. two positive actions they have made that someone else would have appreciated and logged.

DE-BRIEF AND REVIEW:

This will start your training session off on a high and also introduced the topic of the emotional bank account and how it is important that we demonstrate positive actions to others.

Training Support Team

BIRTHDAY GAME

OBJECTIVE:

To learn how to communicate without talking. Helps groups interact quickly with each other and learn something about each other too.

MATERIAL REQUIRED:	TIME REQUIRED:
None	5 - 10 minutes

INSTRUCTIONS:

Ask the whole group to stand up in a straight line.

Then explain to the group that they are to re-arrange themselves in order of birthday (not year) – just day and month from 1 January to 31 December. Tell them though that they are not allowed to speak verbally or write anything down.

Once they are satisfied they are in the right order, ask them to sound off and share their birthdates with the group while in line.

DE-BRIEF AND REVIEW:

ASK THEM

- Was it frustrating?
- How did they manage to do it?
- How could we apply any learnings in our roles?

Training Support Team

DO WE SEE THE SAME THING?

OBJECTIVE:

To help people realise that even though we are subjected to the same stimulus – pictures, smells, sounds, experiences, we often see or react differently. In this case, we are using an image to show this reality.

MATERIAL REQUIRED:	TIME REQUIRED:
Picture of the image shown in the instructions on a piece of paper.	5 minutes

INSTRUCTIONS:

Explain to the group that you will quickly show them a piece of paper with an image on it. Ask them to look at the image and identify what they see. Ask them to keep silent until everyone has seen the image.

Quickly show the image to the left to everyone in the group. Walk round so people get a good look but only for a few seconds.

Then ask the group to say what they saw.

Photocopy or copy the image on the left onto a sheet of paper:

DE-BRIEF AND REVIEW:

ASK THEM

- What did you see? (most people will see either a donkey's head or a seal)
- Can you see in the picture what you didn't originally see?
- How can we apply this in our roles?

Finish the Sentence

FINISH THE SENTENCE

OBJECTIVE:

To help people learn something about each other. To help participants practice thinking on their feet.

MATERIAL REQUIRED:	TIME REQUIRED:
Pen and bits of paper for each person	**10 - 15 MINUTES**

INSTRUCTIONS:

Depending on the group size and how long you want the activity to last, hand out one or two (or more) pieces of paper to each person. The paper should be post it size or smaller.

Instruct the group to write down the beginning of a sentence like:

"My first job was…"

"My favourite hobby is…"

"One thing I'm scared of is…"

Ask them to write legibly as someone else is likely to read it out – but be nice as they may have to read it out themselves. Ask them to fold the paper in half.

Collect all the pieces of paper in a bowl or hat.

Then one at a time, pass the bowl or hat to each person and ask them to take out one of the pieces of paper, read the beginning of the sentence and finish it off

Repeat as necessary.

DE-BRIEF AND REVIEW:

Explain that having something concrete in front of them made it easier to think on their feet.

ASK THEM:

- What did you learn?
- How could we apply this in our roles?

FROG – DOG – MONKEY

OBJECTIVE:

This icebreaker can be used to help break the ice in a fun and relaxed way at the beginning of a training session or meeting.

The icebreaker can be used during training where you want to focus on listening skills or any training session that involves careful attention to sounds.

This icebreaker can also be used as an energiser throughout a training session.

MATERIAL REQUIRED:	TIME REQUIRED:
None	10 – 15 minutes

INSTRUCTIONS:

Prior to starting this icebreaker, the trainer should clearly explain the instructions to the group.

Ask participants to close their eyes (or give them blindfolds) and explain that the icebreaker will be carried out with their eyes closed.

Go around the group and whisper in the ear of the participants one of the following three animals – Frog, Dog or Monkey.

The participants should then make the sound of their own animal i.e. the Frogs would say, 'Gribbit', the Dogs, 'Whoof' and the Monkeys, 'Ooh Ooh'.

The participants should now try and group themselves with their fellow 'animals', using only the sound of their call. They should end up in groups of frogs, dogs and monkeys.

The icebreaker ends when they have achieved the task or the trainer calls a halt to the proceedings.

DE-BRIEF AND REVIEW:

The icebreaker can be reviewed by a discussion of what was important in listening out for the sounds etc. Of course the icebreaker is also a lot of fun and allows participants to relax, have fun and then review the serious points that follow.

GUARD INVADER

OBJECTIVE:

This icebreaker can be used to help break the ice in a fun and relaxed way at the beginning of a training session or meeting.

The icebreaker can be used during training where you want to ensure participants mix and get active.

This icebreaker can also be used as an energiser throughout a training session.

MATERIAL REQUIRED:	TIME REQUIRED:
None	10 – 15 minutes

INSTRUCTIONS:

Prior to starting this icebreaker, the facilitator should clearly explain the instructions to the group.

Ask participants to wander around the room and mingle and mix with each other.

As they are wandering around the room they should look out of the corner of their eye and choose a person that will be their 'Invader'.

Once they have their 'Invader' they should look out of the corner of their eye once more and choose someone to be their 'Guard'.

They should ensure that no one knows who they have picked as their guard or their invader.

Once the facilitator calls the activity to start, the participants must do all they can to ensure that their 'invader' cannot get to them. They do this by trying to ensure their 'guard' is always between them and the 'invader'.

Of course, the result of this activity is that everyone suddenly starts to rush around the room as they try and keep their own guard in the way of their invader. It is great fun as people get squashed into corners and try to avoid obstacles and each other.

Stop the icebreaker when everyone is exhausted or you think they have moved around enough.

DE-BRIEF AND REVIEW:

The icebreaker should be seen as a smooth introduction that gets people to mix and mingle with people they might not have previously.

GUESS WHO

OBJECTIVE:

To break the ice at the start of a training session when participants already know each other.

MATERIAL REQUIRED:	TIME REQUIRED:
Flipchart	15 minutes dependent upon the number of participants
Pen and paper for each participant	

INSTRUCTIONS:

Before starting this activity prime a flip chart with 3 or four questions. Examples may include:

- Favourite film?
- Favourite television programme?
- Favourite food?
- Favourite music?
- Pet hate?
- Famous person you admire?
- Your ideal holiday?
- A unique fact about yourself

Make sure each participant has a blank sheet of paper and a pen or pencil.

Show the prepared flip chart and ask the participants to write their answers on a piece of paper. Tell them to ensure that none of the other participants see the answers they are writing. Allow five minutes for this and then ask participants to fold their answer paper and hand it to you.

Select each piece of paper at random and read out the answers given. Ask the groups to guess who is who.

DE-BRIEF AND REVIEW:

ASK THEM:

- What did you learn during this activity?
- What surprised you?

HUMAN TREASURE HUNT

OBJECTIVE:

This could be used as an icebreaker or as a way to further build trust in a team. It helps people identify things about each other and share about themselves.

MATERIAL REQUIRED:	TIME REQUIRED:
Prepared sheets of paper and a pen for each person	10 minutes

INSTRUCTIONS:

Give everyone a sheet of paper with some prepared items to discover within the group. Each person is to identify someone in the group for each of the items on the list. They should go around the group speaking individually to each other to identify who fits the items on the list. You can make up any list you would like. Here is one to get you started:

Find people in the group who:

- have worked in the business for more than 3 years
- have more than 3 siblings
- have more than 3 pets
- have more than 3 children or grandchildren
- have travelled to more than 3 countries outside of New Zealand
- have seen 3 movies in the last month
- have lived in more than three homes in the last 5 years
- hold more than 3 qualifications

DE-BRIEF AND REVIEW:

ASK THEM

- How would you use that activity in your team?
- What other questions could you include?

INTRODUCTION BY ASSOCIATION

OBJECTIVE:

To help break the ice at the beginning of a training session or meeting.

MATERIAL REQUIRED:	TIME REQUIRED:
None	5 minutes

INSTRUCTIONS:

Explain that this exercise is to help learning by the use of association.

Remind the group that it could be used in a work context if they are having difficulty in remembering something.

Tell the group that they are to introduce themselves to the group by standing up, stating their first given name and associating their name with something they would bring to a picnic.

For example: My name is Fred, and I'd bring some bread.

Possible Variation:

Tell the group they will be asked to introduce themselves to the group by standing up, stating their first given name and associating their name with a personal characteristic that helps identify them, and to do so in the form of a rhyme.

For example: My name is Sue, with eyes of blue.

DE-BRIEF AND REVIEW:

ASK THEM:

- What did they learn?
- Who found that hard?
- How could we apply this to our workplace?

MORNING ROUTINE

OBJECTIVE:

To help people remember then names of others in a group and break the ice of a new group together.

MATERIAL REQUIRED:	TIME REQUIRED:
None	5 - 10 minutes

INSTRUCTIONS:

Get the group to stand up in a circle. In order to help everyone remember each other's names more easily, we're going to add a movement after the introduction.

The facilitator starts and says, "My name is_____ and in the morning, I do this…" and does an action like brushing teeth.

The person next to the facilitator then repeats the facilitator's name and action, then introduces their name and adds a new action by repeating the same phrase: "My name is_____ and in the morning, I do this…" and does an action like washing their face.

The next person goes on but adds the two people that have gone before them and then adds their own – and so on.

DE-BRIEF AND REVIEW:

ASK THEM

- Who would like to repeat everyone's name?
- What did you learn?

NOT MY JOB

OBJECTIVE:

To help team members understand certain frustrations that people have. This could be useful for teams or departments that work together or inter-departmental issues.

MATERIAL REQUIRED:	TIME REQUIRED:
None	5 - 10 minutes

INSTRUCTIONS:

Have everyone in the group stand up and introduce themselves. As part of the exercise, the person is to tell everyone their name and role then to add three things that aren't part of their job.

Give them a couple of minutes to think up three things and allow them to write them down.

People will often share things that they often do that aren't part of their job which will be good for people to hear.

DE-BRIEF AND REVIEW:

ASK THEM

- Were there any surprises there?
- What can we utilise from that exercise back in our roles?

Training Support Team

PAPER AEROPLANE GAME

OBJECTIVE:

To help people get to know each other quickly, have a bit of fun and loosen up at the start of a session.

MATERIAL REQUIRED:	TIME REQUIRED:
Piece of A4 paper for each person	10 minutes (Approximately)

INSTRUCTIONS:

Have everybody in the room write on their piece of paper the following:

Their name

Something they like

Something they don't like

Then have each person make a paper aeroplane out of their paper.

When everyone has finished, ask the group to stand up and move around the room and on the count of three throw their aeroplane across the room.

Explain that after the first throw for the next one minute, they are to pick up any plane near them and throw it across the room. Keep throwing until you call stop.

When you call stop, ask each person to pick up a plane near them. Ensure each person has a plane.

Ask each person to open up the plane, find the person whose name is on the paper and introduce them to the group sharing what they wrote on the plane.

DE-BRIEF AND REVIEW:

Thank them for participating and congratulate them on their plane making skills and their introductions!

PHONE LIFE

OBJECTIVE:

To help the group get to know something about each other quickly. To help the group open up a bit more and build trust. Knowing more about a person can help to build more trust.

MATERIAL REQUIRED:	TIME REQUIRED:
Each person to use their mobile phones	10 minutes (Approximately)

INSTRUCTIONS:

Have each person open up their photos on their mobile phones. Ask them to choose three pictures they will be prepared to share with others that they love, that says something about them or that they're proud of.

Ask the group to pair up and take turns to share the photos they've chosen with someone else. Listen to their story and share yours. Include why you selected those photos and what is the story behind those.

Have them then choose another person to share with and allow a few turns of that.

DE-BRIEF AND REVIEW:

ASK THEM

- What did they learn about each other?
- Did they learn anything about themselves?

PICTURES ABOUT ME - ICEBREAKER

OBJECTIVE:

To help the group get to know something about each other quickly. To help the group open up a bit more and build trust.

MATERIAL REQUIRED:	TIME REQUIRED:
Picture cards	10 minutes (Approximately)

INSTRUCTIONS:

Prepare a pack of picture cards that are eclectic. Include scenery, people, events, food, hobbies, etc. Have the pictures laid out somewhere where people can see them.

Have the group stand up and walk around and ask them to pick two or three pictures that say something about them, represent something they love or are proud about.

Give them three or four minutes to choose pictures and have them return to their seats with them.

Give everybody a time limit - say 30 – 60 seconds and ask them to show the pictures and explain why they picked them.

Consider pinning up the pictures the group chose to remind them of their collective expressions.

DE-BRIEF AND REVIEW:

ASK THEM

- What did they learn about each other?
- Did they learn anything about themselves?

TOILET PAPER

OBJECTIVE:

To help learn things about others in the group.

MATERIAL REQUIRED:	TIME REQUIRED:
Roll of toilet paper	10 minutes

INSTRUCTIONS:

Pass a roll of toilet paper round the group and tell them to take what they need and pass it on to the next person. Don't explain any more than that. If someone asks for clarification, just repeat and say, "Just take what you need". If someone doesn't take any sheets, say to them that they will definitely need at least one – they don't want to be caught out!

When everyone has taken from the toilet roll, explain that as they go around the room, each person must share a fact or something about themselves for each piece of toilet paper they took.

DE-BRIEF AND REVIEW:

ASK THEM

- What did they learn?
- What were they thinking when they were first asked to take what they needed?
- What did they think that meant?
- Is there anything we can apply in our roles?

YEAR OF THE COIN

OBJECTIVE:

To help groups get to know each other quickly and learn something about each other.

MATERIAL REQUIRED:	TIME REQUIRED:
A coin for each person	5 - 10 minutes

INSTRUCTIONS:

Distribute coins for each group or table. Have each member of the group take a coin and read the year it was made. They are to share something related to them and that specific year.

You could ask them to share a brief story by beginning with the sentence: "(YEAR) was a memorable one for me because…"

Have each person in turn share something for their particular year. You could repeat the exercise if needed.

DE-BRIEF AND REVIEW:

ASK THEM

- What did you learn?
- What was the biggest surprise?
- Did anyone learn something about themselves?

ENERGISERS

ARM WRESTLE

OBJECTIVE:

To illustrate the fact that we make massive assumptions and have muscle memory. If we want to change behaviours, we need to change the muscle memory – including our thinking.

MATERIAL REQUIRED:	TIME REQUIRED:
None	5 minutes

INSTRUCTIONS:

Tell everyone to find a partner and get into what appears to be a normal arm wrestling position.

Ask them how many times they can get their partner's hand down. Go!

DE-BRIEF AND REVIEW:

Tell them that when we get into that positon we are usually ready to compete. Ask them:

- Who told you to have an arm wrestle?
- Why did we assume that was the purpose?
- How else could we have approached it?
- How can we apply that to our roles?

BALLOON BUST

OBJECTIVE:

An activity to get the team energized.

MATERIAL REQUIRED:	TIME REQUIRED:
A balloon, piece of string and a roll of newspaper per person	10 – 15 minutes

INSTRUCTIONS:

Give each person in the group a balloon and ask them to blow it up.

Get them to tie the balloon to one of their ankles with a piece of string.

Give the participants a rolled up piece of newspaper.

Explain that each person is to try and pop the other balloons with the roll of newspaper. The winner is the last person left with an un-popped balloon tied to their ankle.

DE-BRIEF AND REVIEW:

ASK THEM

- What plan did they have to win?
- Did they consider attack as well as defence?
- What did they observe around the room?

BLIND ADVICE

OBJECTIVE:

To help the group practice thinking on their feet and deal with interruptions. A great energizer to get the team fired up and ready to go!

MATERIAL REQUIRED:	TIME REQUIRED:
Small pieces of paper and a pen for each person	10 minutes (Approximately)
A hat or bowl	

INSTRUCTIONS:

Give everyone two or three pieces of paper (post-It size). Ask each person to write down a piece of advice they were given when they were younger – perhaps from their parents, a teacher or a friend. Write down one piece of advice per piece of paper. If you need to give them a prompt, suggest something like: "Never talk with your mouth full".

Ask them to fold over the pieces of paper and collect them in the hat or bowl.

One at a time, have each person tell the story of their last week, month or year and get them to pull out a piece of paper and interrupt the story by including what was written on the piece of paper. Have them do one or two each and pass on to the next person.

DE-BRIEF AND REVIEW:

ASK THEM

- How was the activity?
- Was there anything you would change?
- How could we vary it?
- What can we apply to our roles?

CREATIVE STEMS

OBJECTIVE:

To help the group with being creative. A perfect pre-cursor to any brainstorming sessions and great energizer.

MATERIAL REQUIRED:	TIME REQUIRED:
20 Chenille Stems for each group	10 – 20 minutes

INSTRUCTIONS:

Divide the group into small groups of 2, 3 or 4 participants.

Explain that you have been shipped 100,000 chenille stems (pipe cleaners) but the customer cancelled the order and you're stuck with them. There isn't much of a market for them in their current state so the groups must come up with ideas on what they can be used for.

Give them 5 – 10 minutes to come up with some novel ideas then have them present them back to the group.

Consider picking your favourite idea or highlighting your favourite from each group.

DE-BRIEF AND REVIEW:

ASK THEM

- What plan did you have to get started?
- Did you notice how the roles in the group played out?

DING!

OBJECTIVE:

To help the participants think on their feet. This activity will help the group get energized quickly.

MATERIAL REQUIRED:	TIME REQUIRED:
None	5 - 10 minutes

INSTRUCTIONS:

Get the group to divide into pairs. The partners in each pair must now start a conversation about something. Each time the facilitator says 'DING!' they need to say or do something different.

For example, if someone has just said, "I shopped for food" after a DING! They could say, "I shopped for clothes".

If the pair were standing, after a DING! perhaps the then sat down.

You can vary the rules like after a DING!, have the other partner carry on the story or conversation or get them to both do something different and say something different after each DING!

DE-BRIEF AND REVIEW:

ASK THEM

- How was the activity?
- What was hard? What was easy?
- What application could we make in our roles?

DON'T LAUGH

OBJECTIVE:

To help energize a group and lighten the mood.

MATERIAL REQUIRED:

A4 sheet of paper with the word "HA" printed on it

Time Required:

5 - 10 minutes

INSTRUCTIONS:

Get everyone into a circle.

Start with one person in the circle by giving them the sheet of paper with "HA" on it. Ask them to say the word "HA" then pass it on to the next person in the circle. The next person has to say "HA" twice. This continues round the circle with the next person adding a "HA" each time, so a circle of 10 people will have 10 x "HA"s being said.

You can keep going round again adding the 'HA"s. In most cases someone will laugh – then you can start again.

DE-BRIEF AND REVIEW:

ASK THEM

- How does everyone feel?

EARTHQUAKE

OBJECTIVE:

To help the group get energized and up and walking around. It also helps people think on their feet, pay attention and plan ahead.

MATERIAL REQUIRED:	TIME REQUIRED:
None	10 minutes

INSTRUCTIONS:

Tell the group we are going to do an activity.

This game requires the number of participants to be divisible by three plus one extra person – perhaps you as the facilitator are the extra person.

Separate one third of the group as squirrels. The remainder of the group are trees.

Allow them to then get into groups of three – two trees and one squirrel per group.

The two trees form an arch facing each other and have now formed a house. The squirrel crouches under the arch.

The facilitator (or person left out) then has three options. They can call out:

"Squirrels" – at which point, all the squirrels must go and find another house to crouch under

"Trees" – All trees must separate from their tree partner and form another tree over the top of another squirrel

"Earthquake" – Everyone must move into a new position either as a tree or a squirrel!

While any movement is happening, the person in the middle must try and take the place of someone else. The person that is left becomes the new person in the middle and repeats the activity.

DE-BRIEF AND REVIEW:

ASK THEM

- How does everyone feel?
- Did you have a plan for avoiding being the person in the middle?

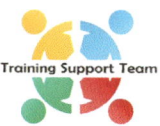

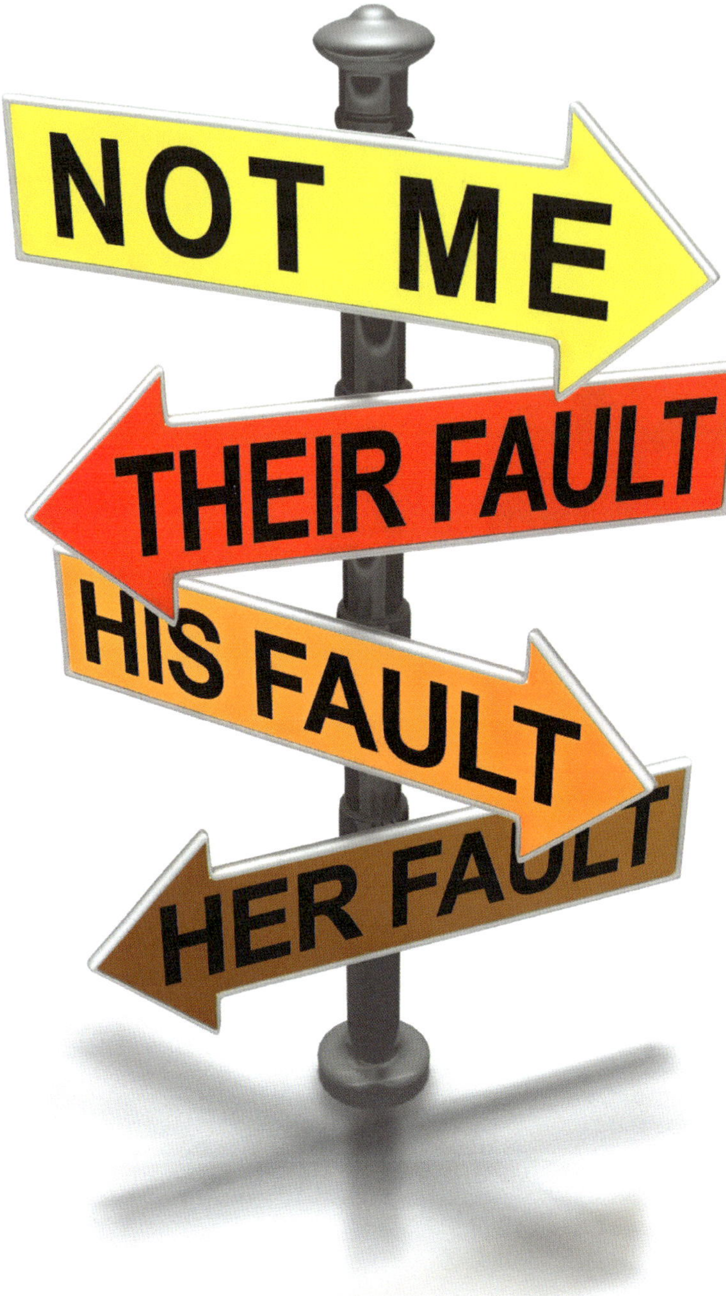
NOT ME
THEIR FAULT
HIS FAULT
HER FAULT

EXCUSES, EXCUSES

OBJECTIVE:

This energizer is a bit of fun and also helps the group to work on creative skills. It can also be a useful activity for problem solving workshops.

MATERIAL REQUIRED:	TIME REQUIRED:
Flipchart or whiteboard and pens	5 - 10 minutes

INSTRUCTIONS:

Provide a list of situations where people will need to provide an excuse such as the following:

- Forgot anniversary
- Didn't do homework
- Assignment is not finished
- Being late to work
- Can't go out
- Didn't get the project done

Ask the group in pairs or threes to come up with the craziest excuses they can for these situations. Give them a few minutes then share them with the wider group.

DE-BRIEF AND REVIEW:

ASK THEM

- How did you come up with the excuses?
- Did you have personal experience?
- Did ideas grow from other ideas?
- Did you have so many you had to choose?
- How could we apply these to our roles?

GOBBELDEGOOK

OBJECTIVE:

To help the group develop creative skills and have some fun. This is an energiser activity to help people get pumped up and ready for work.

MATERIAL REQUIRED:	TIME REQUIRED:
None	10 minutes

INSTRUCTIONS:

Have two people volunteer to role play having a conversation in a made up language. Suggest that they can be quite animated but as they talk, they should make up words that nobody would understand.

Have two other people then act as interpreters. These two people will be interpreting what the other two people are saying.

Suggest that the first two volunteers pause while the interpreters share what they are saying.

Swap out volunteers after a minute or so.

DE-BRIEF AND REVIEW:

ASK THEM

- What was it like to make up a foreign language?
- Did you feel like you were communicating?
- Were the interpreters close to what you meant to say?

INSTANT GAME

OBJECTIVE:

To help people see that they can think on their feet and be creative with minimal planning time. This activity helps to energize a group quickly.

MATERIAL REQUIRED:	TIME REQUIRED:
Whatever is on the tables – pens, toys, koosh balls, paper, etc	10 - 20 minutes

INSTRUCTIONS:

Explain to the group that we are going to invent a new game in each group. This means that in small groups of 2 or 3, each group will use whatever they can find to come up with a new game that will help with a learning need such as:

- Increase product knowledge
- Improve knowledge of the business services offered
- Utilize sales tactics
- Refresh on key learning points from the session
- Help remember the company values

Tell the group they have 3 minutes to come up with a game including the rules. Have them explain the game to the other group members and run the activity. Allow each team to explain and run their activity.

DE-BRIEF AND REVIEW:

ASK THEM

- What did you notice?
- What happened?
- What happened in your group?
- How did the team function?
- When could you use this?
- How could you use your activity to build product knowledge or whatever objective you asked them to focus on?

LONGEST SENTENCE

OBJECTIVE:

To get the group energized and work together well. It also helps the group to think laterally.

MATERIAL REQUIRED:	TIME REQUIRED:
None	5 minutes

INSTRUCTIONS:

Explain to the group that the aim now is to form the longest sentence possible. Divide the groups into tables or small groups of 5 or 6 people.

Have someone say one word to start a sentence and the next person has to carry on the sentence while making sense. It helps to be nice to the next person by not making it hard to follow or forcing them into a full stop as the aim is to make the longest sentence together. Each person adds a new word to the sentence until it naturally ends or no longer makes sense.

DE-BRIEF AND REVIEW:

ASK THEM

- How many words was the longest sentence?
- What strategy did you have to keep the sentence going?
- How could we apply this to our roles?

NAME CHANGER

OBJECTIVE:

To help the group get energized and try to remember the names of the group. This could be used as an icebreaker or an energizer.

MATERIAL REQUIRED:	TIME REQUIRED:
None	5 minutes

INSTRUCTIONS:

Have everybody get up and move into some free space.

Explain that they are to greet a person, introduce themselves and allow the other person to do the same. For example, person A: "Hello, my name is David". Person B: "Hi, my name is Fiona".

Person A then assumes person B's name and vice versa. They then go on to find someone else and introduce themselves using their newly assumed name. They should continue until they get their own name back. They then can sit down.

DE-BRIEF AND REVIEW:

ASK THEM

• Who can remember everyone's name?

QUICK SMILE

OBJECTIVE:

To bring a feeling of positivity in the room. This is a great energizing activity and lots of variations can be made from it.

MATERIAL REQUIRED:	TIME REQUIRED:
Post-it notes for each person	5 - 10 minutes

INSTRUCTIONS:

Give everyone access to post-it notes and ask them to write down something that made them smile today or yesterday. Have someone read out the notes or allow time for everyone to read the notes.

You could dispense with the notes and just have everyone stand up in a circle and share what made them smile today or yesterday.

DE-BRIEF AND REVIEW:

ASK THEM

- How else could you vary this activity with your team?

SAMURAI

OBJECTIVE:

This energizer gets people moving and active. It's a good activity to use when coming back from a break or when people are getting tired. It's also great before heading out on to the retail floor or into a working environment.

MATERIAL REQUIRED:	TIME REQUIRED:
None	5 minutes

INSTRUCTIONS:

Get everybody to stand up in a circle. Explain to the group that we are all Samurai and will be using our imaginary swords.

Start by showing them the movement and explain that you are holding a samurai sword with two hands and will throw your samurai sword from high over your head to someone else in the circle and shout 'HA' as you throw it. The person you throw it to should act like they catch the sword high above their head with both hands. Use big movements.

As the person catches the sword, the two people on either side of them pretend to slash that person with their imaginary swords while also shouting 'HA'. The person who catches the sword then throws it to someone else while shouting 'HA'. The two people either side of the person that catches the sword then pretend to slash that person with their imaginary swords.

Repeat until you feel the activity has done its job.

Encourage the group to use big movements, shout a big 'HA' and watch for their turn to catch, throw or slash.

DE-BRIEF AND REVIEW:

ASK THEM:

- How do we feel?
- Are we energized?

SHAKING HANDS

OBJECTIVE:

To help get people moving and energized. Help with people's concentration skills and coordination skills.

MATERIAL REQUIRED:	TIME REQUIRED:
None	10 minutes

INSTRUCTIONS:

Get everybody to stand up and put their hands out in front of them at chest height.

Explain that there must be three adjacent hands shaking at any one time. You start with both hands in front of you shaking or vibrating. The movement can be like pretending to play the piano. Keep the arms and wrists still.

Explain that because there must be three adjacent hands moving, the person to your right must also start shaking their left hand.

When you stop shaking your left hand, the person next to you must now shake their right hand as well as their left. When you stop shaking your right hand, the person second to your right must start shaking their left hand. Now the person to your right can stop shaking their left hand and the person to their right must start shaking their right hand.

As soon as someone stops shaking a hand, the next hand in the circle must start shaking.

There must be exactly three adjacent hands shaking in the circle at any one time.

DE-BRIEF AND REVIEW:

- Check in with the group to see how they remained in focus.

SWEDISH STORY TELLING

OBJECTIVE:

To help the people think on their feet. This activity will help the participants to see how easy it can be to adjust their thinking when something unexpected happens. It's a good problem solving activity and wonderful energizer.

MATERIAL REQUIRED:	TIME REQUIRED:
None	5 - 10 minutes

INSTRUCTIONS:

Form the group into a circle. If the group is large, you could run this activity as tables.

Have someone start off by telling a story about what they did at the weekend or on holiday or something similar. After a couple of sentences, throw in a random word they need to incorporate into their story. Allow each person in the group to throw in a random word after two or three sentences. Allow each person to have a turn telling a story.

DE-BRIEF AND REVIEW:

ASK THEM

- How did you find that?
- Once you got used to it, could you easily incorporate the random words?
- How could we apply this in our roles?

THE POINTER

OBJECTIVE:

To illustrate that we can always achieve a little more than we first think we can. There's always something we can add to our first effort. This is also a good exercise to do and helps to get the group energized.

MATERIAL REQUIRED:	TIME REQUIRED:
None	5 minutes

INSTRUCTIONS:

Ask everyone to stand up.

Ask the group to place their feet firmly on the floor and remain there for the entire exercise.

Ask them to twist around and point their index finger as far as they can, taking note of where they reached.

Now ask the group to swing their hips and point their index finger and repeat 7 times

Then ask them to swing themselves around 7 times with their eyes facing the opposite direction.

Then a third time with your eyes facing over their shoulders

Now ask them to turn around and see how far you can point. How does it compare with the initial pointing?

DE-BRIEF AND REVIEW:

ASK THEM

- How much further could they point?
- What made the difference?
- How could we apply that to our roles?

THE RIGHT FOOT PROBLEM

OBJECTIVE:

A fun energizer to help people experience a strange phenomenon.

MATERIAL REQUIRED:	TIME REQUIRED:
None	5 minutes

INSTRUCTIONS:

Ask each person to raise their right foot in the air and draw clockwise circles.

While doing this, ask them to raise their right hand and draw the number 6 in the air.

Their right foot will automatically change direction.

DE-BRIEF AND REVIEW:

ASK THEM

- How weird was that?
- What applications are there'?

TWO SIDES

OBJECTIVE:

To illustrate that there are always opportunities to see the positive as well as the negative in any given situation. This helps to focus people on the positive aspects.

MATERIAL REQUIRED:	TIME REQUIRED:
None	10 minutes

INSTRUCTIONS:

Get people into pairs or threes. Have one person share a real life personal or work negative experience. Give them a set time frame of one minute. The other person or people in the team listen.

Then have the same person share the same experience but in a positive light focusing on positive takeaways only. The partner or others in the team also share their positive thoughts on the negative experience.

Get them to swap roles so that everyone one gets to repeat the activity with their own memory of a situation.

DE-BRIEF AND REVIEW:

ASK THEM

- What did you notice about that activity?
- Can you see how there is always a positive from each experience?
- How can we apply this in our roles?

UNFORTUNATELY FORTUNATELY

OBJECTIVE:

To help the group see that there are always two ways to look at things. This is an attitude energizer that helps people think on their feet, get engaged and look for positives.

MATERIAL REQUIRED:	TIME REQUIRED:
None	5 - 10 minutes

INSTRUCTIONS:

Get everyone to form a circle. This works well if there is an odd number. You may want to start and step out if there is an even number of people.

Explain to the group that we will start with a statement and then the first person will say something about that statement beginning with "Unfortunately…". The next person then says something about that last statement beginning with "Fortunately…". You then alternate around the group with "Unfortunately" then "Fortunately". You can keep doing rounds or throw in a new statement.

For example:

Statement: We just bought a new cat.

First person could say: "Unfortunately it isn't house trained yet"

Next person could say: "Fortunately we have wooden floors so it's easy to clean up"

Next person: "Unfortunately I'm the only one at home at the moment so I'm doing all the clean-up."

And so on….

DE-BRIEF AND REVIEW:

ASK THEM

- What does this activity teach us?
- How easy was it to find a contrary statement?
- How can we apply this to our roles?

WAR CRY

OBJECTIVE:

To help the group work together and come up with a war cry anthem they can use to start the day off. This helps unite a team and also energize them both during the activity and every time they use it afterwards. They can recite this right before they go out onto the sales floor, call centre or before visiting customers.

MATERIAL REQUIRED:	TIME REQUIRED:
None	10 - 15 minutes

INSTRUCTIONS:

Divide larger groups into smaller groups of 5 or 6. Explain that they are to come up with a war cry or anthem that they can share with the wider group about them and their roles.

The war cry could be a short tune, a few words involving an action or routine. It should be something that sums up the team and the role they are in. It could incorporate their names or personalities, the company values or vision, how they feel about the business etc.

Give them 10 minutes to come up with the war cry, and then have them share back with the wider group.

DE-BRIEF AND REVIEW:

ASK THEM

- When could they use this?
- How can they implement it?

ZIP, ZAP, ZOP

OBJECTIVE:

To help the group get engaged and up on their feet. It helps people focus and concentrate on what's happening.

MATERIAL REQUIRED:	TIME REQUIRED:
None	5 minutes

INSTRUCTIONS:

Get the group up and into a circle. Explain that there are three words to remember – Zip, Zap and Zop.

Let someone start by pointing at someone else in the circle and say the word "Zip". The person pointed to then points to someone else and says "Zap". That person then points to someone else and says "Zop". The fourth person then starts back at "Zip" and so on. Keep going until someone messes up.

Try going faster and faster to test the skills of the group.

DE-BRIEF AND REVIEW:

ASK THEM

- Who found it difficult?
- How did you stay focused?

ACTIVITIES

AGENDA WALL

OBJECTIVE:

This exercise illustrates the importance of having a clear collective aim for any group, and how poorly a team or organization functions when individuals (or teams within the whole) have different aims within it.

MATERIAL REQUIRED:	TIME REQUIRED:
• A set of bricks per team • The cut up rules per team	30 – 40 minutes

INSTRUCTIONS:

Divide the group into teams. Ensure there are at least 4-6 people per team. Explain that the objective is to build a tower that is the equivalent of 4 standard bricks wide and 15 tall. A standard brick is one with 4 bobbles on it in a row. So the equivalent of 4 of those bricks is what is required.

There can be no gaps in the wall and the wall must be straight and even – ie – no jutting bricks out.

Everyone will receive a rule that they must not discuss with anyone or show anyone – but they MUST ensure that their rule is adhered to while the wall is being built. The teams will empty the blocks and immediately start building.

After one or two rows are up, things will suddenly stop and team members will realize that it is difficult to build because of the rules. Some people will become frustrated and some will try to find some way to share their rules with others. You MUST ensure that the rules are not discussed. People can talk to each other so long as the rules aren't discussed.

After about ten minutes explain to the group that they can eliminate a rule. They can't discuss them but they can vote someone's rule out. That person is still involved in constructing the wall – but without any rule in place.

After a further five minutes, explain to the teams that they can now openly discuss the rules. They should then be able to finish the wall. Notice that some teams may have to re build part of the wall when they realize certain bricks have been used incorrectly or that they need to reclaim certain colours from the wall.

Set of Rules to cut up. One rule per team member and the same set per team:

Your Rules

You must NOT at any time disclose your rules AND still ensure the following conditions are met:

Ensure there are at least FOUR bricks in each row

Your Rules

You must NOT at any time disclose your rules AND still ensure the following conditions are met:

Ensure there are not TWO of the same colour bricks touching in each row

Your Rules

You must NOT at any time disclose your rules AND still ensure the following conditions are met:

Ensure there are YELLOW brick(s) in every other row only

Your Rules

You must NOT at any time disclose your rules AND still ensure the following conditions are met:

Ensure no row contains more than THREE different colour bricks

Your Rules

You must NOT at any time disclose your rules AND still ensure the following conditions are met:

Ensure every row contains at least one BLUE brick

Your Rules

You must NOT at any time disclose your rules AND still ensure the following conditions are met:

Ensure no RED brick touches a BLUE one anywhere

Your Rules

You must NOT at any time disclose your rules AND still ensure the following conditions are met:

Ensure a GREEN brick is at least in every other row

DE-BRIEF AND REVIEW:

Ask them

- How easy was it?
- What did the rules represent? (Agenda, opinions etc)
- What made it easier?
- Whose rule was voted out and why?
- Did everybody get involved?
- How can we apply this at work?

ANTENNAE

OBJECTIVE:

A bit of fun to demonstrate ways we can be more aware of those around us and how we can gel better as a team.

MATERIAL REQUIRED:	TIME REQUIRED:
3 pipe cleaners (chenille stems) for each person	10 – 15 minutes

INSTRUCTIONS:

Hand out 3 pipe cleaners (chenille stems) to each person and demonstrate fixing two together with about ½ inch of each overlapping and twisting round each other. Fix the third one in the same way to create one long pipe cleaner.

Put the pipe cleaners around your head and tie them together at the front and create two antennae. Leave the antennae on your head and encourage everyone to make a pair of antennae themselves and leave them on.

Ask everyone what the things on the head are. The name Antennae should come out pretty easily. Draw a line down the middle of the whiteboard. On the left hand side write "What are these for?" and ask for feedback from the group. Answers will include:

- Feeling
- Sensing
- Checking boundaries
- Giving signals
- Receiving information

On the right hand side of the whiteboard write "What prevents these from working?" and as for feedback from the group. Answer will include:

- Interference / miscommunication
- Noise
- Interruptions
- They break
- Switching off
- No feedback

DE-BRIEF AND REVIEW:

Discuss as a group how these findings can relate as a team, to customers, colleagues, managers, staff etc. Have them come up with ways to avoid the issues that may occur in the right hand column.

APPRECIATION PLATES

OBJECTIVE:

To help people show appreciation for each other in the group. To help everyone feel better about themselves by finding out what the group thinks and appreciates about them. This is a great trust builder and positive esteem builder.

MATERIAL REQUIRED:	TIME REQUIRED:
A pre made appreciation plate (see instructions) for everybody	10 – 20 minutes
Pens for people to write on	

INSTRUCTIONS:

Prepare an appreciation plate for everybody and hand them out. An appreciation plate is a large paper plate with a piece of string or wool threaded through it in two places so that it can hang around someone's neck easily.

Have each person write their name in the middle of the plate and hang their appreciation plate around their necks but ensure they do it so the plate is resting on their upper back. This was so the person can't see the plate.

Now ask everyone to stand up and give everyone a few minutes to go around the room and write something they appreciate about each person on their appreciation plate. Tell them to be helpful and allow others to write on their plates as well as ensuring they write on everyone else's.

When everyone has written something on everyone else's plate, the group can return to their seats, remove the plates and read what has been written about them. The writing should have all been anonymous.

DE-BRIEF AND REVIEW:

ASK THEM

- How did reading the comments make you feel?
- Could you run this with your teams? Families? Where else?

ATTRIBUTE MEANINGS

OBJECTIVE:

To show that we need to be more specific in our communication – especially if the words or phrases are ambiguous or open to interpretation.

MATERIAL REQUIRED:	TIME REQUIRED:
Pen and paper for each person	10 minutes

INSTRUCTIONS:

Explain to the group that you will read out a number of statements and they are to write down what they think each statement means to them. They are to put timings and pinpoint more information to make it clear:

- I'll get back to you in a bit
- I'll load that into the system soon
- Can I come back to you shortly?
- You can only do that a few times
- Lots of people have the same problem
- It's only a minor thing

At the end of all 6, have the group take turns going round for each point to explain what the statement meant to them. You should get varying responses for each point – eg: "a bit" may mean 1 hour, by the end of the day, within a week etc.

DE-BRIEF AND REVIEW:

- Discuss as a group how we can be more specific for these statements and what it will avoid (assumptions, frustrations etc).
- End with saying there are many more phrases we use that mean different things to different people such as "In a timely manner".

BLOCK UP

OBJECTIVE:

Great communication activity that proves that sometimes everyone is right!

MATERIAL REQUIRED:	**TIME REQUIRED:**
Building bricks (Lego or similar) with 3 different colours at least.	30 minutes
Instructions for each of the participants (as described below).	

INSTRUCTIONS:

Participants must build a shared tower using the building blocks provided. Each member of the team is working from their own instructions that the others are not aware of. They cannot talk throughout the activity.

The instructions should be placed on a separate piece of paper for each participant and should either be from the list below or variations on the same theme.

Person 1: Your tower must be fourteen storeys high

Person 2: Your tower must be built with blue and white blocks

Person 3: Your tower must be built with blue, white and red blocks

Person 4: Your tower must contain at least 20 blocks

Person 5: Only you may build the tower

Person 6: The third row of your tower must be blue

The Rules:

Participants must not share their instructions with each other at any point.

Participants must not talk throughout the activity.

DE-BRIEF AND REVIEW:

Have the team rate their effectiveness on a 1-10 scale (1 meaning you didn't work well together, 10 meaning you were extraordinary). They should then comment on their ratings.

- How did they communicate?
- Were there any leaders throughout the activity?
- What difficulties did they face?
- What frustrations, if any, were there?
- How did they feel throughout the activity?
- What worked? What didn't work?
- What would they do differently next time?

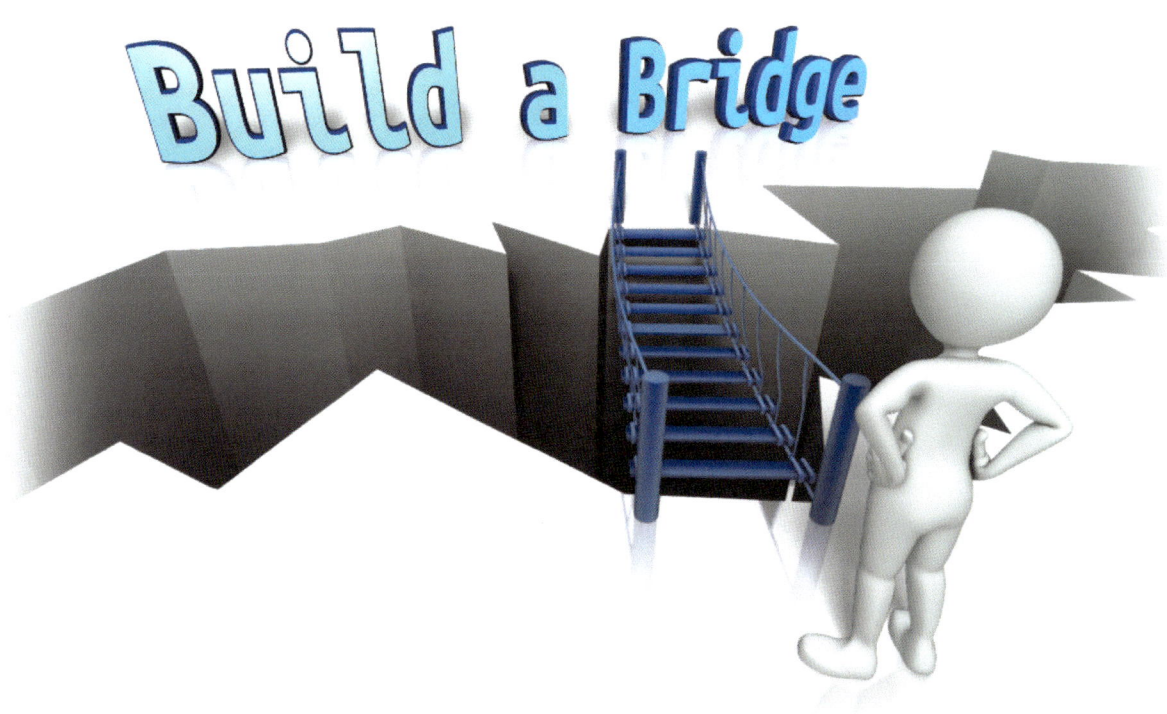

BUILD A BRIDGE

OBJECTIVE:

To illustrate how connected we can become when we contribute or create something ourselves. This will help drive home a connection to things we have ownership for. It will also help people get used to handling LEGO bricks.

MATERIAL REQUIRED:	TIME REQUIRED:
Lego bricks for each person A plastic cup	10 minutes

INSTRUCTIONS:

Provide some Lego bricks or other building blocks for each person.

Tell the group that when you say GO! you would like them to construct a bridge from the LEGO bricks in front of them. Each person must construct his or her own bridge

Tell them the two criteria are:

The bridge must support the weight of a paper or plastic cup

The cup must be able to pass under the bridge

Tell them they will have 3 minutes to complete the bridge.

Go!

Once the time is up, you can ask each person to share something about their model with the group. Use the cup to make sure it can rest on and move under the bridge. There is no penalty for it not working. Choose someone that you will place the cup on their bridge and press down until the bridge collapses

What will happen:

Normally people will separate the bricks to see what they have

Building will start quickly as they are under time pressure

People will ask to try the cup under the bridge to make sure it fits. Let them

The person whose bridge has been made to collapse will be incensed. You didn't say you would push down on it! Allow them to feel the displeasure for a few moments then get into the debrief quickly.

DE-BRIEF AND REVIEW:

ASK THE PERSON YOU CHOSE TO DESTROY THE BRIDGE AND THE GROUP:

- Why did you feel upset when I destroyed your bridge?
- Offer an apology and explain that you were deliberate to make the following point: When we build anything we feel an attachment to it.
- How can we apply this to our work?

CAR OBSERVATIONS

OBJECTIVE:

To illustrate that we can find the good or bad in any situation if we are looking at it.

MATERIAL REQUIRED:	TIME REQUIRED:
Picture of a car	10 – 20 minutes
Pen and paper for each group	

INSTRUCTIONS:

Explain to the group that we will divide the group into two groups (or several groups if there are large numbers). Explain that you will be showing a picture of a car for everyone to see. Assign each group to either identify and write down as many positive things they can find about the car in the picture or as many negative things they can find. A group needs to be specifically aware that they are looking for either positive or negative things.

Give the groups a time limit – like 5 minutes to discuss and write down their lists.

Have the groups share their findings with the rest of the wider group.

Sample car picture to the left.

DE-BRIEF AND REVIEW:

ASK THEM

- What did you notice about the lists of findings?
- How come we could find so many positive and negative things about the same car?
- How can we apply this to our roles? Giving Feedback? Managers? Customers? Our jobs?
- Make the point that if you look for something, you'll probably find it. If you look for something negative, it will be there. If you want to find something positive, you can.

CHANGE PERSPECTIVE

OBJECTIVE:

To help people in the group see things from a different point of view. This activity can be used for any topic or problem solving session.

MATERIAL REQUIRED:	TIME REQUIRED:
Flipchart and pens	10 - 20 minutes

INSTRUCTIONS:

Have a topic that the group needs to discuss. This could be about a process, a product, a situation or something that the group needs to resolve or brainstorm on. For example: Our complaints process.

Have a list of options on the board or have the group come up with a list of potential stakeholders or roles that could be involved or affected by the situation chosen. For example:

- The Manager
- A New Customer
- Biggest Competitor
- Biggest Customer
- Potential New Competitor
- Old Employee
- New Employee

Divide the group into smaller groups of 2 or 3 and get them to brainstorm thoughts based on the role they have been given from the list. Invite the groups to have more than one shot at this by changing the role so they get more than one perspective.

Discuss the perspectives as a wider group.

DE-BRIEF AND REVIEW:

ASK THEM

- Did the role allow you to see things from a different perspective?
- What new ideas came as a result of having a new role to think from?
- Are there any other roles we could include?

What Are Your Thoughts about this New Design for a Coffee Cup?

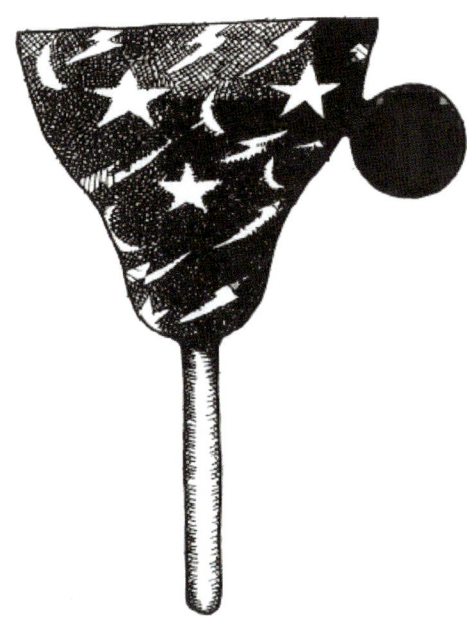

THE COFFEE CUP

OBJECTIVE:

To help people see their natural reactions to change. To help identify that we shouldn't make assumptions and ask more questions before passing judgements.

MATERIAL REQUIRED:	TIME REQUIRED:
Picture of the coffee cup.	10 – 15 minutes
Pen and paper for each participant	

INSTRUCTIONS:

Show the slide with the new design for a coffee cup:

Ask participants to write down 3-4 reactions/ thoughts/observations they have to this.

Ask for a few reactions and once you hear one, ask, "Who else had a similar response?"

Ask participants to put:

- A minus sign (-) next to those observations that were negative.
- A plus sign (+) next to those that were positive.
- A (0) next to those that were neutral, like "It's black."

Ask for a show of hands, "Who had more positive responses than negative or neutral responses?"

"Who had more neutral than positive or negative?"

"Who had more negative than neutral or positive?"

DE-BRIEF AND REVIEW:

After the counting, say, "If this group resembles most groups, there will be more negative than positive or neutral responses. Why? Because the new design does not match what we have in our brains when we hear the words 'coffee cup.' This one is not a match for what we know."

Explain that this new design for a coffee cup is simply a metaphor for how we tend to react to something new, to a change. As humans, we tend to criticize or judge first, with words such as, "That will never work."

In fact, this coffee cup is designed for the beach --- to stick in the sand! If someone were to come from a mindset of curiosity, they might wonder, "Is this designed to be used in a specific situation?"

ASK THEM:

- How can we apply this in our roles?

COUNT TO 20

OBJECTIVE:

To return a group to a calm state. This is an opportunity for a group to get in tune with one another. It's an opportunity to be aware of what's happening around them.

MATERIAL REQUIRED:	TIME REQUIRED:
None	5 minutes

INSTRUCTIONS:

Gather the group together and have them either sit down, stand in a circle or even put hands on shoulders in a circle.

Explain that as a group we are going to count from 1 to 20.

The rules are that we will all close our eyes; only one person must say a number at a time and only one number at a time. Anyone can say the next number. If more than one person speaks at one time, we will start back at number 1 again.

Take your time and one person start the counting.

DE-BRIEF AND REVIEW:

ASK THEM

- How does everyone feel?
- Do you feel calm?
- Are you relaxed?
- How do we feel as a group?

FOLDING PAPER

OBJECTIVE:

To illustrate the point that even with the same instructions, people will interpret them differently. Clarification around instructions is vital to ensure people understand exactly what is meant by them.

MATERIAL REQUIRED:	TIME REQUIRED:
Piece of A4 paper for everyone	10 minutes

INSTRUCTIONS:

Give everyone a sheet of paper.

Tell everyone to close their eyes and follow your instructions.

Start giving instructions about what to do with the piece of paper examples:

Fold it in half

Fold the lower left corner over the upper right corner

Turn it 90 degrees to the left

Rip a half-circle in the middle of the right side

Turn the paper upside down

Tear off an inch from the top of the paper

Fold it again

…Add a couple more instructions

Once you have given the instructions, tell everyone to open their eyes and unfold their piece of paper.

Even though they all received the same instructions and had the same starting material, pretty much everyone will have a different result.

DE-BRIEF AND REVIEW:

AREAS TO DISCUSS AND SHARE WITH THE GROUP:

- We don't all start with the same base (some held their piece of paper vertically or horizontally) so we don't all have the same results
- Some interpreted to rip a piece of paper as removing a big piece, some as a small piece
- Having eyes closed = not receiving feedback on our performance
- Some instructions appear vague to some and clear to others.
- Many other conclusions can be drawn on the fly from this

FOX, CHICKEN, GRAIN

OBJECTIVE:

To help the group problem solve and think about the one solution to a particular challenge.

MATERIAL REQUIRED:	TIME REQUIRED:
None	10 minutes

INSTRUCTIONS:

Divide the wider group into smaller teams – pairs or threes. Explain the scenario below:

A farmer has bought three items in a village and now needs to transport them across the river on his boat. The three items are: a fox, a chicken and a bag of grain. The issue is that he can only fit one item in his boat with him at a time. He has to be careful because he can't leave the chicken with the grain as it will eat it and he can't leave the fox with the chicken because the fox will eat the chicken.

How can he get his three items across the river in his boat?

Give the teams a few minutes to work through the problem and then ask for a solution.

Solution is: The farmer takes the chicken over in the boat and leaves it on the other side of the river. He goes back and picks up the fox. He then drops off the fox but takes the chicken back with him and leaves the chicken while he takes back the grain. He then goes back for the chicken.

DE-BRIEF AND REVIEW:

ASK THEM

- What was your thinking process?
- Have you heard of it before?
- Is there any other option?
- How can we apply this in our roles?

GIVING SPECIFIC INSTRUCTIONS

OBJECTIVE:

To show that when we give instructions or feedback to somebody, we need to be specific. Specific feedback will help someone make correct changes to get the required result.

MATERIAL REQUIRED:	TIME REQUIRED:
• 3 koosh balls	10 minutes
• A bin	
• A blindfold	

PREPARED SHEETS WITH PHRASES AS DESCRIBED IN THE INSTRUCTIONS

INSTRUCTIONS:

Ask for two volunteers.

Once you have them, tell one they will be blindfolded and will be asked to throw three koosh balls into a rubbish bin held by the other person.

Tell the person holding the bin not to say anything at any time and not to move the bin to help catch the balls.

Prepare some sheets of paper and ask the group to shout out these phrases only after the person throws each koosh ball whether they get it in the bin or not:

"Well done"

"You nearly did it"

"At least you had a go"

"Nice try"

Spin the person who is blindfolded around once or twice and ask them to throw the koosh balls.

After the person has thrown the koosh balls, ask them if the group had helped them at all with their words?

Give the blindfolded person another three koosh balls and this time, ask the group to say whatever they want to help the thrower get the balls in the bin.

Hopefully at least one ball will make it in to the bin.

DE-BRIEF AND REVIEW:

Thank the two volunteers and ask them to be seated. Ask the group what was different between the two throwing sessions. Draw out that the second session allowed for direction to be given. Although the first session comments were encouraging, they didn't actually help the person correct their behaviour in order to target the bin more accurately.

THE GREAT EGG DROP

OBJECTIVE:

To see how teams work together in a short space of time under pressure, allocate tasks and agree on a final outcome for success.

MATERIAL REQUIRED FOR EACH TEAM:	TIME REQUIRED:
75cm of tape	30 minutes
20 straws	
1 raw egg	

INSTRUCTIONS:

READ OUT TO THE GROUP:

Your group represents one of many business groups that are vying for a very lucrative contract for miniature communications beacons.

The contract will be awarded to the Hi Tec group who develops a fail-safe delivery system for dropping an egg, using the least amount of materials.

The essential and final criteria for success is an intact egg at the end of product testing. This is particularly significant when you realise that your successful design will establish structural guidelines for air drops of the highly sensitive communications beacons into strategic locations around the country.

The actual device is very similar in weight and dimension to a raw egg with a similar sensitivity. CELL TEC and other agencies are seeking a FAIL SAFE delivery system using cheap resources such as straws and tape which do not require the use of expensive parachutes.

In addition to d esigning your product and in keeping with modern marketing practice, it must be given an appropriate commercial NAME and you will be expected to deliver a creative, promotional pitch highlighting the features and benefits of your design.

Your pitch will be given in front of all other competing delegates.

Your egg delivery system will then be test dropped from a height of 2 metres onto a firm surface to simulate the wilderness terrain. Remember finishing early and using less materials helps make your product look better to the buyers and the project team not to mention the JUDGE! BUT the essential criteria is a WHOLE egg after the drop!!

You will be given the following construction materials:

- 75cm of tape
- 20 straws
- 1 raw egg

You may NOT use any other materials

INSTRUCTIONS:

TIMING:

You will be given 15 minutes in which you must:

- Come up with a name
- Come up with a marketing pitch
- Build your device

WHAT WILL HAPPEN:

The teams will be planning how to build the safest egg holder. They will be trying out methods of fixing straws together and of conserving tape.

You may need to remind them to come up with the marketing pitch and the name of the product if they don't get started on those 10 minutes in to the activity.

Once the 15 minutes is up, have each team deliver their pitch and drop the egg device containing the egg on to a flipchart pad or similar to ensure the egg doesn't splatter everywhere on carpet. You will judge the name and pitch and score as follows:

SCORING:

- 15 points for a complete egg after the drop
- 5 points for a cracked egg
- 0 points for a broken egg
- Up to 5 points for the marketing pitch
- Up to 5 points for the Product name
- 1 bonus point for each straw unused up to 5

DE-BRIEF AND REVIEW:

ASK THEM

- How long did the planning last?
- Could everyone share the vision of the finished product?
- What were the key factors in coming up with the design?
- What are two things you could have done better?
- What are two things you did really well?
- What learnings can we apply to work?

HEADACHE ACTIVITY

OBJECTIVE:

To illustrate what type of questions we need to use to gain information, the different responses we receive when using different questions and the importance of listening to the customers' responses. This activity also shows how long a situation can go on for when a scattered approach is used for questioning versus a structured approach.

MATERIAL REQUIRED:	TIME REQUIRED:
None	20 – 25 minutes

INSTRUCTIONS:

Explain to the group that when you say go, you want them to get into two teams and that we are going to have a quiz.

Explain to the group that they are doctors and their task is to diagnose what is causing my headaches and how to avoid them for the future. DO NOT go down the medical route as they don't know enough and also it is not medically related.

Rules of the game: Each team gets a chance to ask one question at a time, If your team asks more than one question I will only answer one of them; if you cannot think of a question your team can pass

You have 10 minutes planning time to list all the questions you want to ask.
At this point discreetly get a folder and draw up a page to record number of open questions and closed questions (It is important that the group do not know what you are recording at this stage)

Only respond to the type of question the group has asked i.e. if they ask a closed question respond with a yes or no – if they ask an open question, answer with that detail required – do not give extra information

When you start the activity, before they plan the questions – begin with: "I have a headache and I would like you tell me how to avoid it happening in the future" - let them plan then you can start by repeating the question and alternate between the teams, recording open and closed questions on your sheet of paper.

Other Details you need to know and provide – only if the question is asked:

Had headaches for the last 3 months

Get them on a Sunday afternoon and they go by Monday mid-morning

Your job is a trainer

You started new hobbies about 3 months ago which are (make some up such as oil painting, motor mechanics, photography AND community work) They will think elements in the hobbies are giving headaches such oils or chemicals in photo's etc. Must include the community work.

You help out and go to church every Sunday morning – Only say this when you are asked directly what your community service is OR what you do on a Sunday morning

You help out at church by ringing the bell – Do NOT tell them this one unless asked what you do

INSTRUCTIONS:

at church!

What will happen:

- The groups will split and begin listing their questions. Due to the time constraints they will not be able to list all of the questions they need to ask to find the answers. When they run out of questions they will AUTOMATICALLY switch to closed questions (every group does!).
- They will give you a scattered approach to the questions
- They may compete with the other team by NOT sharing questions and not following from each other's questions
- They may not listen to the other group and therefore ask the same questions the other team has
- They may begin to get frustrated when they cannot seem to find answers (at this point stop them and review the facts for them)

DE-BRIEF AND REVIEW:

Explain to the group the need to have a plan of all the critical information they need and then format the questions to obtain this information in a timely and structured manner

Explain what happens if we jump to conclusions – we get the wrong answer or can confuse the customer, longer call times etc.

As you progress through the activity people will jump in and TELL you what's wrong before they know!!!

Draw up on the flipchart category headings and ask what categories could we have listed our questions under.

TIMEFRAME   HEALTH   HOBBIES   CHANGES   WORK

How different do you think the activity would be if we had asked our questions like this as opposed to the shotgun / scattered approach??

HELIUM STICK

OBJECTIVE:

To help teams work better together and communicate effectively.

MATERIAL REQUIRED:	TIME REQUIRED:
A broom handle or similar	10 minutes (Approximately)

INSTRUCTIONS:

Get the group to line up in two rows facing each other and Introduce the Helium Stick to them (show them the broom handle).

Ask participants to point their index fingers and hold their arms out.

Lay the Helium Stick down on their fingers. Get the group to adjust their finger heights until the Helium Stick is horizontal and everyone's index fingers are touching the stick.

Tell the group that they need to lower the Helium Stick to the ground. However, explain that each person's fingers must be in contact with the Helium Stick at all times. Pinching or grabbing the pole is not allowed - it must rest on top of fingers.

If anyone's finger is not touching the Helium Stick, the task will be restarted.

Okay, Go!

WHAT WILL HAPPEN:

Near the beginning, the group will find that the Helium Stick will tend to rise and float up rather than lower. This will cause some laughter from the group. As the facilitator, you can add to this by asking what on earth they are doing. You're supposed to be going down.

Some groups may be tempted to give up because it's too hard. The facilitator can offer direct suggestions or suggest the group stops the task, discusses their strategy, and then has another go.

Occasionally, a group may appear to be succeeding too quickly. Ensure you are keeping an eye and making sure the fingers are all touching the pole. Also make sure participants lower the pole all the way onto the ground.

Eventually the group needs to calm down, concentrate, and very slowly, patiently lower the Helium Stick.

DE-BRIEF AND REVIEW:

ASK THEM
- What did you think as you started the activity?
- What skills did it take to be successful?
- What suggestions were made and how were they received?
- What roles did people play?
- What did each group member learn about him/her self as an individual?
- What other situations are like the Helium Stick?

Training Support Team

HOW MANY FS?

OBJECTIVE:

To illustrate that the brain often misses things it initially sees. Pointing out that we need to look more closely at things in front of us.

MATERIAL REQUIRED:	TIME REQUIRED:
A copy of the statement in the Instructions for each participant	5 - 10 minutes

INSTRUCTIONS:

Hand out a copy of the statement to everyone or have them already on the chairs before you start.

Explain that each person has a special piece of paper with a statement on it. Tell them to read the statement and count how many letter 'F's they can find in the statement.

Give them a minute and then ask for all the people who had 4 Fs to stand up, then 5 Fs and then 6 Fs. Finally ask those with 7 Fs to stand up. People will think they had different sheets.

Here is the statement to copy for everyone.

FINISHED FILES ARE THE RESULT OF YEARS OF SCIENTIFIC STUDY COMBINED WITH THE EXPERIENCE OF MANY YEARS OF EXPERTS.

DE-BRIEF AND REVIEW:

ASK THEM

- Did you realise you all had the same sheets?
- Count the Fs again and how many can you find?
- What does this activity say about you? About a short sentence and how we didn't all find the right number? What else are we easily overlooking?

IDOL

OBJECTIVE:

To illustrate that people are watching even the smallest actions we make. This activity can be a fun energizer and help get the group moving and engaged.

MATERIAL REQUIRED:	Time Required:
None	5 minutes

INSTRUCTIONS:

Get everybody to stand up and form a circle. Ask for the youngest (or oldest) person in the circle to raise their hand. Ask them to point to another person in the circle. Now ask that person to point to someone else and repeat until everyone is pointing at someone and has someone pointing at them. Keep the people pointing to make sure this is the case.

Now get the people to drop their hands and just look at that person. Tell them that for the remainder of the activity they are just to look at that person only. Explain that the person they are looking at is their Idol.

Now, when you say go, everyone must stand still unless their idol does something and then they must copy everything that their idol does. They mustn't do anything unless their idol does it. If their idol laughs, they must laugh. If they twitch, they must twitch and so on.

Okay, Go!

After a few seconds, there should be a relay of movement happening. Someone will do something even though they are supposed to only copy their idol. Movements will become more exaggerated. If you see nothing happening, walk around and remind them that they must copy their idol. Point things out if necessary.

After a minute or so you can stop the activity and quickly debrief and then have another go.

DE-BRIEF AND REVIEW:

ASK THEM

- Who started the movement? You were supposed to only move if your idol did.
- Do we like to find someone to blame for setting of the reaction?
- How small were some of the movements? Did we notice them?

Explain that even small movements can be observed. We may not notice what we are doing or think that anyone else is watching but someone will be.

Ask them

- How can we apply this to our roles?

IMPERFECTION

OBJECTIVE:

To help people see that you don't always have to strive for perfection to get a point across or to help people understand. This activity is good for time management sessions in particular but could be used anytime you want a fun activity that links to putting in too much effort when a simpler approach will do.

MATERIAL REQUIRED:	TIME REQUIRED:
A4 sheet of paper and pen for half the group	10 minutes
Flipchart paper and stand	

INSTRUCTIONS:

Prepare a flipchart in the room and cover up the words so no one can see. Organise the group so half of the group can see the flipchart paper once the words are revealed and the other half to sit opposite so they can't see the flipchart side with the words on.

Prepare the flipchart with words like the following:

- Apple
- Square
- Rectangle
- House

- Chair
- Circle
- Tree
- Lightbulb

- Triangle
- Person

Explain to the group with the A4 sheets that you will reveal a list of words one at a time but fairly quickly and they are to draw a representation of the word on their paper. Give about 5 – 10 seconds between words as you reveal them. It will be good to cover the words with another piece of flipchart paper and slowly reveal each word as you go. Don't make the time too long as you want people to do a rough sketch only.

Once you have finished revealing all words, have the people with the drawings give their paper to someone on the opposite side and ask these people to guess what each of the pictures are.

The group should be able to guess the objects drawn even though they will be rough sketches. Reveal the words to all participants.

DE-BRIEF AND REVIEW:

ASK THEM

- How many objects could you guess correctly?
- Would it have made much difference if the 'sketchers' had much more time to do more detail?

Make the point that we don't need to overdo somethings. If we are short on time, stick to the basics. Sometimes we do a job over and above the expectation required and as a result may lose time, frustrate customers, miss out on doing other work etc.

Training Support Team

INCORRECT RESPONSE

OBJECTIVE:

To help participants think laterally and recall specific training points or product knowledge. It helps people have to concentrate and pay attention as well as be creative.

MATERIAL REQUIRED:	TIME REQUIRED:
None	10 – 20 minutes

INSTRUCTIONS:

Explain that we will be doing a recap of the session so far (or focus on products or services of the company).

The rules of this activity are that you must keep the subject relevant to the session (or company products or whatever you have designated the boundaries to be).

As the facilitator, you start by asking a question and invite people to give an incorrect answer but still relevant to the session. Someone else then has to ask a question that the previous answer would be correct for.

Some examples if the session was all about colours:

QUESTION: What is one of the colours on the English flag?

ANSWER: Purple

QUESTION: What is the colour of a blueberry?

ANSWER: Pink

QUESTION: What finishes this sentence: "Pretty in…."

ANSWER: White

QUESTION: What colour is snow?

ANSWER: Black

QUESTION: What ball is worth 7 points in a game of snooker?

And so on.

DE-BRIEF AND REVIEW:

Review the answers given and the questions to make sure they were correct. Give people a chance to correct any mistakes. Check after a couple of rounds to make sure people aren't confused.

IS THIS A TEAM?

OBJECTIVE:

To help the participants identify what makes up a team and the difference between a group, set of individuals and a team.

MATERIAL REQUIRED:	TIME REQUIRED:
None	5 - 10 minutes

INSTRUCTIONS:

Ask 2 participants to stand.

Question to the group: Are they a team? Why not? (They're just 2 individuals)

Ask another 3 participants to stand (previous 2 remain standing)

Question to the group: Are they a team now? Why not? (They're a collection of individuals and are not standing together)

Ask the 5 individuals to move to the front and stand together.

Question to the group: Are they a team yet? (No, they are a group of people)

Question to the group: What is lacking to make them a team?

Possible answers:

- No clear common purpose
- No task to work towards
- No goals or objectives
- They share only a common interest which is to do this exercise

Ask a member of the group standing to leave the room. Assign a task to those members remaining, e.g. to count the number of slats in the blinds in the room.

Question to the group: Are these people standing here and the person outside a team now? Why not? (No, one member is missing and they're not working together OR yes but one person doesn't know the task yet. In a high performing team, all members need to know the task and how they can contribute to the completion of it.

Recall the outsider and ask them: How do you feel? Are you part of a team? (Might feel left out, not know what's going on)

Tell the outsider what the task was

Question to the group: Who would accomplish the task quicker, all these people working as a team or the individual working alone? (The team working together utilising each other's strengths and skills as they can accomplish more working as one unit)

Thank the group and allow them to return to their seats.

DE-BRIEF AND REVIEW:

ASK THEM

- What's the difference between a team and a group of individuals?

- How would we now define a team?

- What makes a team potentially more effective than an individual?

JIGSAW PUZZZLE

OBJECTIVE:

To illustrate what can happen if we are / are not proactive when we reach a difficult area in work. To help staff understand that by being proactive when an issue arises they can work through it and complete tasks rather than waiting for a solution.

MATERIAL REQUIRED:	TIME REQUIRED:
TWO jigsaws (small size – ie 24 pieces) with similar pictures and one or two pieces from the middle of each picture swapped so the jigsaw cannot be completed with the pieces given.	15 - 20 minutes

INSTRUCTIONS:

Prepare two bags of jigsaws with a centre piece swapped over in each jigsaw so that the puzzles can't possibly be completed unless they work together.

Explain to the group that when you say go, you want them to get into two teams and that we are going to have an activity

Pass each group a bag with jigsaw puzzle pieces in it. Explain that one team is responsible for completing one jigsaw and the other team is responsible for completing the other jigsaw.

Tell them to start and then just observe the team behaviours while completing the activity.

NO TIMEFRAME is GIVEN but you can walk around looking at the groups and glancing at your watch (make sure some of each group see you doing this)

What will happen:

The groups will rush in to start putting the jigsaw together. Most will start with the corners and then the outside edges and they will usually make the frame much bigger than they need to for all the pieces to fit in.

They will realise the frame is too big and bring the pieces in closer but then not be able to finish the picture as some of the pieces do not fit in the middle.

Some members will start to complain they don't fit and then look around for guidance, some may even ask the trainer and the trainer must just shrug and say they have everything they need to complete the task, some will just sit back and give up, some will automatically look at the other team to see if they are the same and if they are they may talk to them and swap pieces.

DE-BRIEF AND REVIEW:

ASK THEM

- What plan did you have for your task?

- How many just jumped in started without any discussion or planning?

- When completing tasks you will face obstructions or issues. The key is to be proactive and find solutions – how does this relate to your job?

- Communication is a great problem solver – what would have happened if neither team had told the other they were having problems with their jigsaw?

- If they had to complete the task again knowing what they know now would the task be completed faster? WHY? How does this relate to the tasks you undertake every day at work?

Explain that the group needs to be proactive – this may be seeing an issue before it arises; such as a delay or missing information, being proactive with the customer and have good communication to keep them informed of progress or missing items just like the jigsaw.

LIFE SHIELD

OBJECTIVE:

To help everyone get to know each other in the group well and to provide a good grounding of positive energy in a working group. Help teams share appreciation for each other in an anonymous way.

MATERIAL REQUIRED:	TIME REQUIRED:
Flipchart sheet and pens for each person	30 minutes

INSTRUCTIONS:

Explain that everyone in the room will be completing a life shield and show them an example of what it will look like on a screen or prepare one on a flipchart pad like this:

Explain that they are to draw a shield to cover their flipchart sheet and then complete as follows:

On the left hand side, write their name.

On the top right box write something they are proud of or passionate about

On the second box on the right, write down their biggest challenge currently they face in their role

On the third box on the right, write done something they would like to get out of the workshop / session they are in

On the fourth box on the right, write down something they are looking forward to in the future

You may like to give examples as you go.

Finally, ask them when they have completed their own shield, they are to write something in the left hand box of everyone else's shield other than their own. They should write something positive about that person and why they are good value.

As a variation, you could provide pictures for them to choose from to show what they are proud of or passionate about and provide blu tac to have them stick them up on their shields.

DE-BRIEF AND REVIEW:

Once everyone has completed their own shield and everyone has written something on everyone else's shield, gather them all together and one by one go to everyone's shield, have the person whose shield it is explain the items on the right and hand side and you read out the items on the left.

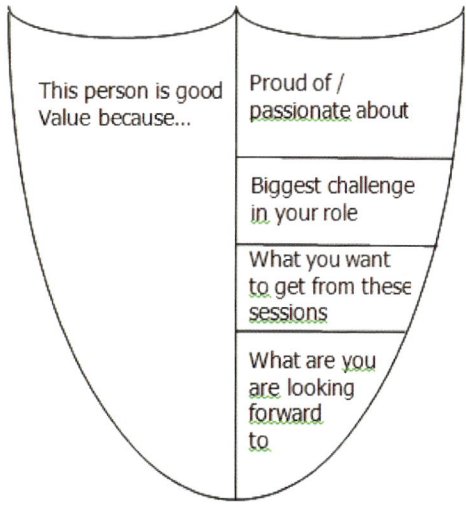

LISTENING QUIZ

OBJECTIVE:

This activity demonstrates how we listen through preconceived ideas. We take information we already know and automatically and often apply it to a situation which looks in this case sounds familiar. THIS IS FOR FUN only and should not be taken too seriously.

MATERIAL REQUIRED:	TIME REQUIRED:
Pen and paper for each person	10 minutes

INSTRUCTIONS:

Explain to the group that it is time for a listening quiz.

This is to be completed on your own and if you know the answers please do not call them out

"On the left hand side of the page write down 1 to 8"

Wait…

See if any participants have written 128 and how many have written 1234….8. Note the instruction and how easy it is to get communication wrong!

Get everyone to write in full 1-8

Explain you will only read out the questions once and you will not repeat them.

Any questions before I start?

Number 1

A man builds a square house and all sides face south, a bear comes to the door and rings the doorbell. What colour is the bear?

Number 2

You walk into a COLD DARK room and in the COLD DARK room you see a candle, a kerosene lamp, an oil heater, and fire place with paper and kindling. (say this bit quickly) You have one match in your matchbox, which do you light FIRST, for maximum HEAT?

Number 3

 (say this first part quite quickly) You are the driver of a bus. (Now normally) You leave the bus terminal at EXACTLY 6.57am, at the first stop you pick up 3 men, 3 women and 4 children. At the second stop you pick up 2 children, drop off the women and pick 1 more man. At the third stop you pick up 2 women drop off 2 children and 2 men. At the fourth stop you drop off all the men, pick 3 women and 2 more children.

This goes on all morning until you get back to the bus terminal at EXACTLY 11.57am.

(Pause)

What colour is the bus drivers eyes?

Number 4

According to INTERNATIONAL law when a plane is travelling from one country to another and it crashes on the EXACT border between the countries, according to INTERNATIONAL law where are the survivors buried, in the country they are coming from or the country they are going to, according to INTERNATIONAL law?

Number 5

It's been raining for forty days and forty nights, the rains and floods have come. GOD tells a man to build a large wooden boat and save as many pairs of the animals as he can.

How many pairs of animals did Moses take on board the Ark during the great flood?

Number 6

Can a man marry his widow's sister – yes or No?

Number 7

Do they have a fourth of July in England?

Number 8

Can a man living in Australia be buried in NZ?

Number 9

There are 3 apples and you take away 2 how many do you have?

DE-BRIEF AND REVIEW:

The aim is to show how quickly we can become confused, misdirected or just switch off when it gets too hard to listen.

Go back through the quiz and show where the misdirection took place and why (some people may need to be given the answers again as it may take a while to click!)

Answers are:

White – it's a Polar Bear (Only place you can build a house with 4 sides facing South is the North Pole)

The MATCH!!!

Whatever your eyes are – opening sentence YOU are the driver of a bus!

We don't bury survivors….

It wasn't Moses, it was Noah (people hear the opening and jump to conclusions)

NO – if she is a widow then he is DEAD

YES of course they do; after the 3rd and before the 5th!!

No, Because he is LIVING….

2 BECAUSE you took of them

LISTENING SKILLS

OBJECTIVE:

To demonstrate peoples listening skills and how easily they are distracted either by outside influences or by their own thoughts.

MATERIAL REQUIRED:	TIME REQUIRED:
Pen and paper for each person	10 minutes

INSTRUCTIONS:

Tell everyone they will have to write EXACTLY what you read out – BUT they cannot begin writing until you have FINISHED reading out each phrase and you tell them begin.

At the end they will swap their papers with the next person and score each other's answers.

Check everyone has working pen and clean sheet of paper. They are to number each phrase 1 – 5.

Read the following phrases clearly and concisely but only read them out ONCE!! Ensure no-one starts writing until you have finished reading each one out. Get them to write out each phrase after you have read it (not all five at once). Check everyone is finished the current one before you move on.

Read out the following phrases:

Gerry said there were 28 pencils and 30 red pens in the blue truck

Please tell Martin to add two thousand and 42 dollars and 29 cents to Jim's expense account on Monday the 23rd

Ask Bill to bring 24 application forms and 76 pens to the introductory meeting tonight

After you have cleaned the bathroom please take care to put the broom back into the closet and the bucket back under the sink

When I say you there is no I, and when I say I there is no you

Now check the answers. They must be EXACTLY the same as you read out!

What will happen:

People will struggle to get the answer EXACTLY right as they will forget details, hear different things or get distracted and miss words.

DE-BRIEF AND REVIEW:

ASK THEM

- "That was easy wasn't it?"

They will give you responses along the lines of NO etc!!!

Explain that the same thing happens when we are speaking with customers, which is why we must ensure we WRITE notes as we go, we must be engaged and we must paraphrase to ensure we get it right.

ASK THEM:

- What plan did you have for trying to remember each phrase?
- Were some more difficult than others?

MATCHING PAIR

OBJECTIVE:

To help the group practice asking the right types of questions and to effectively communicate.

MATERIAL REQUIRED:	TIME REQUIRED:
• Pre made papers with pairs of things cut up	10 – 15 minutes
• Tape	

INSTRUCTIONS:

Pre prepare some papers with some paired objects on them.

Pairs like: Salt and Pepper, Sun and Moon, Night and Day, Yin and Yang, Bread and Butter etc.

Separate the pairs of papers and tape a piece of paper with one item written on it to the back of each person in the room.

Each person must then go around the room and ask Yes/ No questions to try and find out what they are and pair up with the person that has the correct pair to their paper.

DE-BRIEF AND REVIEW:

ASK THEM

- How did you change your approach during the activity?
- What tactics worked?
- What did you learn about communication?
- How can we apply this in our roles?

MEMORY TEST

OBJECTIVE:

To help participants discover basic psychological facts about our memory. It's a fun activity that can be used for any number of people.

MATERIAL REQUIRED:	TIME REQUIRED:
Pen and paer for each participant	10 – 15 minutes

INSTRUCTIONS:

Tell them that you are going to administer a memory test. You will read a standardized list of words. Participants should listen carefully to these words without writing them down. Later, you will test to see how many words each participant can recall.

Present words. Read the following list of words. Pause briefly between one word and the next. Do not change the sequence. One of the words (night) is repeated three times:

Dream	sleep	night	mattress	snooze	Sheet
nod	tired	night	artichoke	insomnia	blanket
night	alarm	nap	snore	pillow	

Administer the recall test. Pause for about 10 seconds. Ask each participant to take a piece of paper and write as many of the words as he or she can remember. Pause for about 40 seconds.

Explain your intent. Reassure participants that you are not interested in finding out how each person performed on the test. Instead, you are going to use the test to explore four basic principles about memory.

DE-BRIEF AND REVIEW:

Here are four important principles about memory. Explain each of them, using data from participants' performance on the test:

- Primacy and recency effects. Ask participants to raise their hands if they recalled the words "dream" and "pillow". Explain that people remember the first and the last things in a series. Most participants will have written dream and pillow because they were the first and last words in the list.

- Surprise effect. Ask participants to raise their hands if they recalled the word "artichoke". Explain that people remember things that are novel or different. Most participants will have written artichoke because it is different from the other words in the list.

- Repetition effect. Ask participants to raise their hands if they recalled the word "night". Explain that people remember things that are repeated. Most participants will have written night because you repeated it three times.

- False-memory effect. Ask participants to raise their hands if they recalled the word "bed". Reveal that this word was not on your list. Explain that the brain closes logical gaps in what it hears, sees, or reads, frequently remembering things that did not take place. Most participants will have written bed because it logically belongs to this list (even though you never read it).

Encourage action planning. Ask participants how they would use these four principles to help them remember new terms and ideas in the training session. Give examples such as, "To compensate for the primacy and the recency effects, pay particular attention to ideas presented during the middle of the training session. Make use of the repetition effect by repeating these ideas to yourself several times."

MONUMENT ACTIVITY

OBJECTIVE:

To illustrate the power of questioning techniques and how we often get consumed with what we want to sell when we should be asking questions and uncovering the customer's true needs / wants, thus making the presentation to the customer highly effective.

MATERIAL REQUIRED:	TIME REQUIRED:
Lego blocks or similar for each team	20 minutes (Approximately)

INSTRUCTIONS:

Split the group into 3-4 teams (3-4 people in each team) and have them go to their respective tables (lots of lego blocks are required for each team)

Explain to the group the following: I am the wealthiest person in the world and I've topped Forbes riches 100 list for the past 10 years. I'm extremely vain and want a Monument built (bit of humour) the largest most extravagant monument, the king of monuments, a monument that makes the Eiffel tower look small.

You are all monument construction project companies and are vying to get my business, therefore you're not only going to build the monument of / for me, you're also going to sell it to me!

I'm going to tell you my requirements, and I'm only going to tell you twice so listen carefully!

You'll have 10 mins to build this monument and when you're finished one of your team will act as the sales person.

- The monument has to be big
- The monument has to be tall
- The monument has to be extravagant
- The monument has to be earthquake proof (tell the group that you will be going around and shaking the tables presales! Therefore they better test it out before their sales presentation)

Those are all of your requirements however reinforce the BIG, TALL, EXTRAVAGANT! AND IT'S FOR ME!

NOW REPEAT THE INFORMATION

READY, GO!

Things you don't tell the participants (unless asked when you're walking around):

- You've recently been diagnosed with an incurable disease, hence you want the monument built
- You hate the colour red!
- Your favourite colour is yellow, hence your favourite flower is a sunflower! (it would be great if they can incorporate this into the monument)

Start the exercise and walk around, don't say anything unless they speak to you first, however some groups might say "what do you think?" if the question is closed and non-specific always reinforce "big, tall, extravagant, and EARTHQUAKE PROOF! Tell the groups in 3-4 min intervals "make sure it's earthquake proof! TEST! TEST! TEST!"

If they ask specific open questions, then answer them

Once the time is over have a member of their team sell the monument to you.

Test the monument's to ensure that they are earthquake proof.

Judge the winner and debrief.

What will happen:

As you wander around the room don't say anything, you will notice everyone working very hard to make the biggest and tallest monument which is earth quake proof.

Usually no one ask questions so reinforce the big, tall, earthquake proof.

DE-BRIEF AND REVIEW:

While everyone is still in their teams ask:

- "What was your plan?"
- "How did everyone feel about the 10 minutes to build?"
- "What testing procedures did you implement?"

Ask them:

- What do you think this exercise was for?
- Who was this monument for? What were my requirements? Was that all my requirements? Why didn't anyone ask me further questions?

Most people will say, the exercise was all about planning, organising, and project management. However tell them, it was about the customer, what did the customer really want? How often do we get caught up in our own processes and procedures, when we should be focussing on what the customer wants, and without questions we do not uncover the customer's true needs! Remember, NO CUSTOMER NO JOB! Are you truly customer centric?

MULTITASKING

OBJECTIVE:

To illustrate what can happen when we try to do more than one thing at once.

MATERIAL REQUIRED:	TIME REQUIRED:
A pen and paper for each participant	10 – 15 minutes
Stopwatch or watch	

INSTRUCTIONS:

Explain to the group that you will be asking them to write down two lines of information on a piece of paper.

You may want to demonstrate on a whiteboard what you mean. Tell them to write the sentence "Multi-tasking disengages the brain." On one line, then write out the full alphabet underneath on the next line:

"Multitasking disengages the brain"

"abcdefghijklmnopqrstuvwxyz"

Using a watch or stopwatch record each person's time to completion.

Now, write the sentence again only this time as you write each letter of the sentence you drop down and write a letter of the alphabet underneath.

E.g. M (write 'a' below the 'm'), u (write 'b' below the 'u'), i (write 'c' below the 'i'), t (write 'd' below the 't') etc.

Using a watch or stopwatch time each person to completion again.

What will happen:

The first sentence and alphabet will be done quite quickly. People usually do it in approximately 30 seconds.

The second attempt is much harder to do.

Some people will give it a go through to the end.

Others will give up in frustration and confusion.

Their writing and accuracy will deteriorate the second time.

DE-BRIEF AND REVIEW:

ASK THEM

- What was the difference between the two attempts?
- How easy was it to concentrate each time?
- What difference was there in the time taken to complete the two tasks?
- Was there a change in quality?
- Do you habitually multi-task?

Explain that this is what happens when we try to multi-task at work, at home and when driving.

Multi-tasking is not effective.

MY ROLE

OBJECTIVE:

An activity to help the group see everyone's role from their own perspectives. It's a great way to communicate with the team and explain about their role from a visual perspective.

MATERIAL REQUIRED:	TIME REQUIRED:
Either LEGO bricks or flipchart paper and pens for each person	20 - 30 minutes

INSTRUCTIONS:

Explain that everyone will have 5 – 10 minutes to either build with LEGO or draw on a flipchart (you choose which medium to use – or you could let each person choose) a representation of their role.

The build or drawing should incorporate the following:

They can use metaphors, analogies from movies, sports or any other methods of describing what they do.

Once the participants have finished, bring the whole group together. Invite each person to tell the story of their picture or build. Ask the group to see how each fits into the wider view of the team and what it does.

DE-BRIEF AND REVIEW:

ASK THEM

- How do you see your role?
- How does your role fit in with the bigger picture?
- How does your role relate to other jobs in the room?
- Having seen other people's pictures or builds, has your perception changed?

ONE WAY COMMUNICATION

OBJECTIVE:

To demonstrate the many problems that can occur in one-way communication.

MATERIAL REQUIRED:	TIME REQUIRED:
Pen and paper for each person	10 – 15 minutes
A prepared diagram for one participant	

INSTRUCTIONS:

The group is going to experiment with directions as they are involved in one-way communications.

Select someone to be the person giving the instructions to the group. They will be holding the paper and describing the drawing to everyone else.

Each member of the group will then listen to the instructions and redraw what they are being described. Participants must not ask questions or give any verbal responses. The person giving instructions cannot ask questions of the group either and should not be able to see the participants.

A sample diagram to follow could be like this:

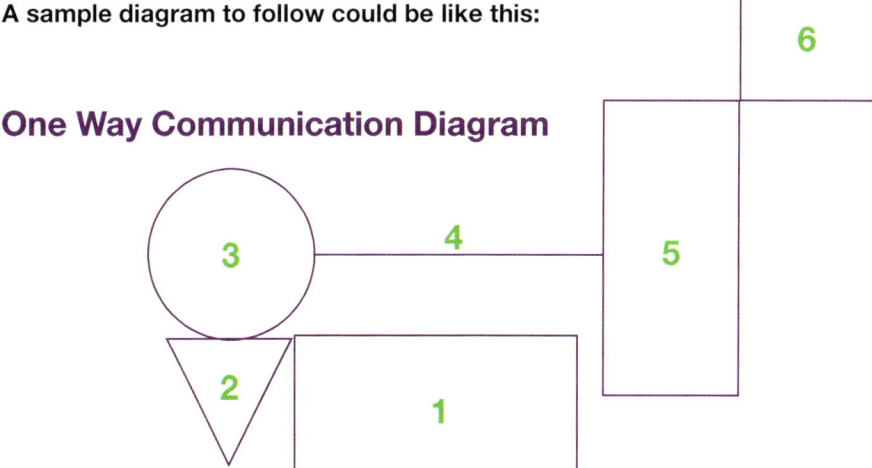

When the person explaining the drawing has finished, show the participants the drawing and allow them to compare drawings.

DE-BRIEF AND REVIEW:

ASK THEM

- Why was one way communication difficult to follow?
- What would have made it easier?
- How can we apply that in our roles?

PAPER TOWER

OBJECTIVE:

To help the group work together to form an objective. Communication skills, team work and some logic thinking are all required.

MATERIAL REQUIRED:	TIME REQUIRED:
4 sheets of A4 paper per team	20 - 30 minutes
4 paperclips per team	
Measuring tape	

INSTRUCTIONS:

Divide the wider group into teams. 3 – 6 people per team works well.

Explain that each group will be given a set of materials and their aim is to build the tallest, free-standing structure from those materials only.

They will have 10 minutes to plan and build.

Materials for each team:

4 sheets of A4 paper and 4 paper clips.

Go!

When the time is up, get everyone to step away from their towers. Measure the towers to determine the winner. Ensure no other materials have been used and that the tower is free-standing.

DE-BRIEF AND REVIEW:

Ask the groups to spend two minutes reviewing their experience and come up with two things they feel they did really well and two things they would do differently if they were to do the exercise again. Share with the wider group.

ASK THEM:

- What did they learn?
- What could they apply back to their roles?

PARACHUTE GAMES

OBJECTIVE:

This is a couple of fun activities designed to help participants experience the practice of working together to achieve an agreed outcome.

MATERIAL REQUIRED:	TIME REQUIRED:
• A bed sheet or towel	10 minutes (Approximately)
• 1 x ball	
• A selection of toys	

INSTRUCTIONS:

Ask the group to stand in a circle around a parachute (the bed sheet or towel) and have each person hold the edge in front of them so that the parachute is off the ground. You can then engage in one of the following two games.

Ball Bungee – Place a ball in the middle of the parachute and ask participants to work together and see how high they can flick the ball up into the air.

To me, to you – Place a ball in the middle of the parachute and ask participants to take it in turns to work the ball towards one of the team. Once it reaches that person, they must select a new person to roll the ball towards. You can make this activity more difficult by using toys rather than balls as they will not roll as easily.

DE-BRIEF AND REVIEW:

Have the team rate their effectiveness on a 1-10 scale (1 meaning you didn't work well together, 10 meaning you were excellent). They should then comment on their ratings.

ASK THEM:

"What would you have had to do to rate your teamwork a 10?"

PICTURE CARDS

OBJECTIVE:

To help a group share and understand more about each other in certain situations. Help the group be able to tell a story through the use of available picture cards.

MATERIAL REQUIRED:	TIME REQUIRED:
Picture cards	10 – 15 minutes

INSTRUCTIONS:

Provide a selection of picture cards as photos or images. Have them laminated so they are durable and can be re-used. Spread the picture cards on a table or provide the group with a pile of them to sort through.

You can create many variations of this activity. Consider some of these examples while asking the group to sift through the cards:

Choose a picture card / photo that describes what sort of day / week you had

Select a card that reflects your goals for the week

Choose several cards and form a collage with the people in your team that reflects excellence in customer service

Form a collage that reflects one of our business values

DE-BRIEF AND REVIEW:

ASK THEM

- What did you learn from the activity?
- What other questions or situations can you come up with?

PLANT ANIMAL NAME

OBJECTIVE:

To help participants in the group to get to know each other. This exercise is spread over part of the day so keeps people thinking.

MATERIAL REQUIRED:	TIME REQUIRED:
None	5 - 10 minutes then 20 minutes later

INSTRUCTIONS:

Ask everyone in the group to think up a name for themselves based on the following:

- Their new first name must be a plant, vegetable, flower or tree
- Their new second name must be an animal, fish or bird

For example: – Hyacinth Husky (They don't have to begin with the same letter)

Explain to them that they will need to be able to explain why they have chosen their particular name later in the day, but that they must not let the other participants know what they have chosen yet.

The chosen names should be written on a piece of paper, which in turn should be handed to you.

Explain that you are going to write each name up on flip chart paper and display them around the room, and that during the day you would like everyone to write the name of the person that they think is represented by the plant animal name.

You can also use this activity at suitable points in the day to raise energy levels by inviting participants to take a minute or two to walk around the room and add to the flip chart sheets.

Choose a point in the day to lead the group in revealing who is who, what their colleagues thought, and why each person chose their particular name. You could share the name and share who thought they were then have the actual person reveal who it really was and why they chose the name.

DE-BRIEF AND REVIEW:

This is an opportunity to get to know each other well. Thank them for participating. Ask if anyone would choose different names next time and why.

PLAYING CARDS

OBJECTIVE:

To help Improve leadership, team-building, problem-solving and communication skills

MATERIAL REQUIRED:	TIME REQUIRED:
2 packs of playing cards per team	10 – 20 minutes

INSTRUCTIONS:

This simple team exercise requires two decks of cards per team with different distinctive coloured backs for each team. Remove the three of spades from one of the decks of each team and store them in an envelope ahead of the exercise. Shuffle the two decks for each team in advance of the activity and place them face up on a different table for each team. (Ensure the teams do not see that the backs are different styles.) Split group into teams of between four and seven people in each team. Do not allow teams to go near the tables at this point. Ask one member from each team to step out of the room. The facilitator then explains to these individuals that their responsibility is to pass on the instructions for the exercise to their teams. Do not mention leadership or that they are leaders in any way.

EXPLAIN TO THE TEAM MEMBERS VOLUNTEERING TO RECEIVE INSTRUCTIONS:

The purpose of the task is as follows. Your team has two separate decks of cards which I want you to sort into suits and display 'ace-high', i.e. aces facing up on the top of the piles followed by king, queen, etc., down to the two, which should be at the bottom of each pile. You should have eight piles at the end of the activity. You need to tell me that the task is correct and complete when you are finished. Are there any questions? Return to the room and inform groups not to talk until told.

Allow the individuals to re-join their teams. Look at your watch, pause and say 'start now'. Wander between the groups and keep looking at the watch which should be in your hand rather than on the wrist.

TIMING:

Allow them enough time to complete the task – but don't give them a set time.

What will happen:

Teams will start immediately and organise themselves. When they realise the 3 of spades is missing they may mention it or just carry on with the task and hope it's okay not to have them. The cards if different backed colours may all be mixed.

DE-BRIEF AND REVIEW:

Observations guide for facilitator - points to review after the activity:

Use of physical resources - Were the teams able to gather around the table and if not did they reposition it?

Human resources - How well were team members involved in the task? Did each have a role to play, and if not why not?

Time - There was no time limit given. Did they feel there was one? Was this due to body language? Did anyone ask about time?

Competition - Did the teams feel it was a competition between teams and if so why? What about collaboration? If the teams did not know that the exercise was a competition then why did the first team to finish not help the remaining teams to complete the activity? Was the missing card identified? Was the information shared with all members of the team? Did teams inform you at the end of the exercise?

Cards - Were the decks separated first by turning them over so the backs were visible or were the decks mixed up? If so why?

Passing on of information and seeking clarification - Did the initially selected representatives assume the role of leaders? Did an expert leader emerge because for example they play cards or did leadership rotate.

Type of leadership - What type of leadership was exhibited? Facilitative, autocratic, democratic, etc., encourage the teams to discuss this.

You will see other aspects to review, depending on your situation and what happens during the activity. While this team exercise is quick to play, the discussion and review can take longer. There are very many aspects of team-working, collaboration, assumptions, communications, leadership, etc., to explore. You can also encourage the teams to discuss their experiences in their teams and relate what happened to what happens in the workplace when working in teams.

Training Support Team

POOR CUSTOMER SERVICE

OBJECTIVE:

To help participants understand both what to say and what not to say in customer service situations. It helps people to be able to rephrase their statements in a positive way.

MATERIAL REQUIRED:	TIME REQUIRED:
None	10 - 15 minutes

INSTRUCTIONS:

Form a circle with the participants and as the facilitator, you stand in the middle of the group. Explain that each person will have an opportunity to rephrase a poor customer service statement and come up with another poor example.

The first person in the circle is to come up with a phrase that is not right and should not be said to a customer such as, "You don't know what you're talking about".

The next person in the circle is to then change the wording of the statement in a positive way such as, "Thank you for sharing your thoughts".

That person then comes up with a negative example of a phrase you should never say to a customer and the next person must rephrase positively.

Don't allow too much time to think and move on to the next person if they struggle.

DE-BRIEF AND REVIEW:

ASK THEM

- Which negative phrases have you used in the past? What about the positive ones?
- What do you think the effect of these negative statements could be on customers?
- Which phrase was easier to come up with under pressure – negative or positive?
- What key piece of learning will you take away from this activity?
- What can we apply in our roles?

PRESSURE COOKER

OBJECTIVE:

To help the group understand the difference between pressure and stress and identify ways to avoid creating stress in their lives.

MATERIAL REQUIRED:	TIME REQUIRED:
A whiteboard	10 – 15 minutes
A pretend list of names of participants	

INSTRUCTIONS:

Ask the group what they think is the difference between pressure and stress. Get a few responses and then explain that you'd like to illustrate something for them.

Explain that you have a list of all their names in front of you and that you will randomly pick one and ask them to come to the front and recite a nursery rhyme (or something similar).

Close your eyes and pretend to pick a name at random from an imaginary list. Open your eyes, look down at the list and say: "We're not going to do that".

You will hear sounds of relief from the group!

Explain to the group that they were, at that moment, all under the same pressure. However, some of them had turned it into a stressful situation. Some would be worried they couldn't think of a nursery rhyme, others may even be secretly hoping to get picked as they like the limelight. Whatever they felt, the pressure was the same, and it's what they all did with it that may have turned into stress.

Pressure is external and Stress is internal. The three main stress areas are:

Internal Stress: Worry

Environmental Stress: Noise, Crowds, Work

Chronic Stress: Overworked, too much going on at school, fatigue

Explain that it's really good to have an outlet for stress. Explain that our lives are like a bucket and stuff keeps going into the bucket. At some point the bucket will overflow – that exhibits itself as anger, crying, meltdowns etc. So in order to let stuff out, we need to punch some holes in the bucket. (You can draw the bucket as you go here).

What are some holes that you can punch in your bucket to relieve some stress?

Ask the group to discuss in small groups and share some thoughts.

It's important to understand our own stress relievers for our health's sake.

DE-BRIEF AND REVIEW:

ASK THEM

- What can you do to avoid these three types of stress?
- If you have one of them surface, what can you do to avoid overflow?

QUESTIONING SKILLS

OBJECTIVE:

To illustrate the power of questioning techniques and how difficult it can be to think of questions when you are not prepared.

MATERIAL REQUIRED:	TIME REQUIRED:
3 pens for each person	10 minutes (Approximately)

INSTRUCTIONS:

Tell everyone to pick up three pens from the table. It doesn't matter what three pens they are.

Have the group split up into pairs and spread out round the room.

Tell them they to have a CONVERSATION using only questions BUT they are not to answer the question with an answer but with ANOTHER question.

Every time you answer a question you lose a life (one of the three pens) the winner is the person in the pair with the most pens!

CORRECT EXAMPLE: (It must flow as a conversation)

"How long have you worked for ABC company?"

"Is it important for you to know that?"

"What is it about the question you don't want to answer?"

"If I answer you will you stop asking'?" Etc etc

INCORRECT EXAMPLE:

"How long have you worked for ABC Company?"

"Do you enjoy your job?"

"What do you like about your job?"

"What do you do here?" Etc etc.

DE-BRIEF AND REVIEW:

ASK THEM

- What plan did you have for your questions?   .
- How many open questions versus closed questions did you ask?

Training Support Team

RIGHT NOW

OBJECTIVE:

To help the group understand how they are feeling and how others are feeling right now in the moment.

MATERIAL REQUIRED:	TIME REQUIRED:
Building blocks for each person	10 – 15 minutes

INSTRUCTIONS:

Give everybody some building blocks. These can be a small bag or a pre-purchase set. Enough for at least 10 – 20 blocks per person. LEGO bricks are deal.

Ask the group to build a quick model out of the blocks that represents how they are feeling right now about one of the following:

- The session they are in
- Their role
- This week
- The business
- Or something along those lines.

Give them 2 or 3 minutes only to build.

Then have each person share back with the group what they have built and what it represents. Ask them to take just 30 seconds each to share. For larger groups, you may want to divide them into groups of 6-8 maximum.

DE-BRIEF AND REVIEW:

ASK THEM

- How could they use this activity with their teams?
- Can they think of any other variations?

ROOM IMPROVEMENT

OBJECTIVE:

To illustrate that goals and objectives are important and should be set or clarified before engaging in action.

MATERIAL REQUIRED:	TIME REQUIRED:
The seating in the room	10 minutes

INSTRUCTIONS:

Tell the group that they will have exactly one minute to improve their seating arrangement. Don't give them any other details and tell them that their time starts now. Go!

If anyone asks for clarification, just repeat the initial instructions. If people push for more, just tell them to work out for themselves what "improve" means.

After one minute elapses, tell the group to stop.

DE-BRIEF AND REVIEW:

ASK THEM

- Did you meet your objective?
- What was your objective? What did "improve" mean?
- Did anyone try to clarify? What happened?
- How can we relate this to our workplace or roles?

SEARCH THE ALPHABET

OBJECTIVE:

This exercise can be used to explore how diverse we are and gather insights into ourselves. If done as a small group it lends itself well to a small team building exercise as the group works together through the alphabet.

MATERIAL REQUIRED:	TIME REQUIRED:
None	10 minutes

INSTRUCTIONS:

Divide the participants into small groups.

Explain that as a group they are to search their person for objects that they have on them or with them ranging from A-Z.

Have them make a list.

Explain that the first group to get all 26 letters represented wins.

Go!

DE-BRIEF AND REVIEW:

ASK THEM

- What plan did you have for winning the game?
- How inventive did you get with the letters?
- How could we apply this to our roles?

SHOPPING LIST

OBJECTIVE:

To illustrate that the tone of voice makes a difference when talking with someone and how easy it can be to identify someone's tone.

MATERIAL REQUIRED:	TIME REQUIRED:
Whiteboard and pen	10 - 15 minutes

INSTRUCTIONS:

Explain to the group that we need to build a shopping list of a few things we may get from the supermarket. Get them to call out the first 5 things and then add something funny like: Toilet Roll.

Your list may end being something like:

- Bread
- Milk
- Cereal
- Toothpaste
- Chocolate
- Toilet Roll

Then ask the group to call out some types of voice tones we may experience. They can be things like: Angry, frustrated, happy, excited, nervous, seductive etc

Write a few up on the board.

Now ask the group to get into pairs and take it in turns to read the shopping list out to each other in one of those tones you have listed on the board – but the must do it facing away from each other – no eye contact.

Ensure both people in the pair have had a turn and ask each person to guess which tone the speaker was using. They should read out the entire list in the same tone. If time allows, get them to try a couple of times each.

DE-BRIEF AND REVIEW:

ASK THEM

- Were you able to guess the tones used?
- What tones do we hear our customers or colleagues use?
- How easy is it to tell?
- How did we adjust our responses dependant on the tones we hear?
- How can we apply this to our roles?

SPAGHETTI TOWER

OBJECTIVE:

To see how teams work together with a simple project. Can they follow instructions and find the most efficient way to complete a task for the least amount of cost.

MATERIAL REQUIRED:	TIME REQUIRED:
• 20 pieces of spaghetti • 1 metre of scotch tape • 20 marshmallows • 1 Small plastic cup • PLUS a measuring tape (one only for the whole activity)	15 minutes to build + De-brief and introduction time (25 minutes total)

INSTRUCTIONS:

100 years ago, in big cities, the tallest buildings were made of brick and could only be a few stories tall. That's because the brick was so heavy, buildings couldn't support their own weight if they were too high.

As cities became more crowded and the building space ran out, the only way for buildings to get bigger was to go up ... so, building designers had to figure out a way to do this. They came up with a way to give the building a kind of supporting skeleton, made of steel beams. Then bricks and other building materials could be used to cover the outside of the building and it wouldn't fall down. These new structures were so tall they seemed to "scrape the sky"... so they were called skyscrapers.

In this activity, you will have 15 minutes in which to construct a skyscraper using pieces of spaghetti, mini-marshmallows and masking tape. The problems that you and your team-mates must solve are:

- How to make the tallest tower possible within the time limit.
- How to make the tower sturdy enough to stand alone.
- How to make the tower strong enough to hold the weight of a small paper cup.

While you are doing this, you might also consider some architectural issues, such as:

Which shapes are stronger? Triangles? Squares? Pentagons? The pieces of spaghetti are used to build the tower and will cost $1 each. You can use whole pieces, half pieces or whatever, but even if you use just a small fraction of a piece, it will still cost you a buck. Marshmallows are used for tower connections and will cost you $1 apiece. Scotch tape can be used to tape the base of your tower to the desk or anywhere else on the tower. You have 1 metre of tape and each 10 cm of tape will cost you $1 as well.

Give each team a copy of a sheet showing the following to do their own calculations:

RECORDING SHEET FOR SPAGHETTI TOWER ACTIVITY

TEAM NAME:

TOWER NAME:

Building Costs:

Pieces of spaghetti used _____ x $1 =

Cost: $

Marshmallows used _____ x $1 =

Cost: $

Each 10cm of tape used _____ x $1 =

Cost: $

Total Cost: $

Our tower was _____ cm tall (divide by this number).

Total Cost per cm: (Cost / Height)_____

Supplies:

20 pieces of spaghetti...$1.00 ea

20 mini-marshmallows...$1.00 ea
1 metre of tape ....$1.00 per 10 cm

DE-BRIEF AND REVIEW:

ASK THEM

- Was everyone involved?
- How did the teams plan?
- What would the teams do differently if they could do it again?
- Did the teams elect a leader?
- Did everyone agree?
- Was their sufficient time allocated to planning?
- How can we apply this to our working environment?

SUNGLASSES ACTIVITY

OBJECTIVE:

To illustrate the power of questioning techniques and how difficult it can be to think of questions when you are not prepared.

MATERIAL REQUIRED:	TIME REQUIRED:
A pair of sunglasses	5 - 10 minutes

INSTRUCTIONS:

Put on a pair of sunglasses and just look around the group.

Ask the group who wears sunglasses from time to time.

Ask the group why they change sunglasses (They break, get lost, go out of fashion, get scratched)

Focus on the scratched lens. That's what you see when you put on those sunglasses – it obscures our view somewhat. Explain to the group that in our lives, we see things in a particular way – like wearing sunglasses. During our life we pick up scratches on our lenses due to experiences we have:

- We get a boss – all bosses are like them – scratch on the lens
- We meet someone from America – all Americans are like them – scratch on the lens
- We get asked to do a project – all projects are like that – scratch on the lens
- We speak to a customer who has English as a second language – all those who have English as a second language are like them – scratch on the lens

DE-BRIEF AND REVIEW:

- It's not until we take off the sunglasses that we see more clearly. So, occasionally, take off those sunglasses of life and look at things without a pre-determined view or prejudice. It can make all the difference when dealing with customers and colleagues.
- What are some prejudices we may have with customers? Colleagues? Suppliers?
- How can we overcome those prejudices?

Training Support Team

SUPERHERO

OBJECTIVE:

A team working activity that can be used as an energizer, during induction or any time you want a group to work together and come up with some ideas to solidify a particular topic or the values of an organisation.

MATERIAL REQUIRED:	TIME REQUIRED:
Flipchart paper and pens for each group	30 minutes

INSTRUCTIONS:

Divide the wider group into smaller groups. You can have 2 to 8 participants in a group. Explain that each group has 20 minutes to invent a superhero with a theme based on the values of your organisation. You can vary this by talking about products or services or another set of parameters that suit your session.

Here's what they need to include:

- As a group come up with a name for their superhero
- Design and draw an outfit
- The superhero must have three special powers (for example – invisibility or flight)
- Put together a mission statement for the super hero

At the end of the time, allow each group to introduce their superhero to the wider group.

DE-BRIEF AND REVIEW:

ASK THEM

- Did everyone feel involved?
- Did anything stop them from working effectively?
- Would they change anything if they did it again?

SURVIVAL SIMULATION

OBJECTIVE:

Helping a group work together to come to a consensus. This activity helps to identify different roles in a group and what is needed to come to a collective agreement.

MATERIAL REQUIRED:	TIME REQUIRED:
Handout of survival equipment	20 - 30 minutes

INSTRUCTIONS:

You and your companions have just survived the crash of a small plane. Both the pilot and co-pilot were killed in the crash. It is mid January, and you are in Northern Canada. The daily temperature is 25 below zero, and the night time temperature is 40 below zero. There is snow on the ground, and the countryside is wooded with several creeks criss-crossing the area. The nearest town is 20 miles away. You are all dressed in city clothes appropriate for a business meeting. Your group of survivors managed to salvage the following items:

- A ball of steel wool
- A small axe
- A loaded .45-caliber pistol
- Can of Crisco shortening
- Newspapers (one per person)
- Cigarette lighter (without fluid)
- Extra shirt and pants for each survivor
- 20 x 20 ft. piece of heavy-duty canvas
- A sectional air map made of plastic
- One quart of 100-proof whiskey
- A compass
- Family-size chocolate bars (one per person)

Your task as a group is to choose the 5 most important items from list the above, place them in order of importance for your survival and explain why you chose them. You MUST come to agreement as a group. You have 20 minutes to decide.

DE-BRIEF AND REVIEW:

ASK THEM

- How were decisions made?
- Who influenced the decisions and how?
- How could better decisions have been made?
- Did people listen to each other? if not why not?
- What roles did group members adopt?
- How was conflict managed?
- What kinds of behaviour helped or hindered the group?
- How did people feel about the decisions?
- How satisfied was each person with the decision (ask each participant to rate his / her satisfaction out of 10, then obtain a group average and compare / discuss with other groups' satisfaction levels)
- What have you learnt about the functioning of this group?
- How would you do the activity differently if you were asked to do it again?
- What situations at work/home/school do you think are like this exercise?
- How many open questions versus closed questions did you ask?

Explanation for the group:

Mid-January is the coldest time of year in Northern Canada. The first problem the survivors face is the preservation of body heat and the protection against its loss. This problem can be solved by building a fire, minimizing movement and exertion, using as much insulation as possible, and constructing a shelter.

The participants have just crash-landed. Many individuals tend to overlook the enormous shock reaction this has on the human body and the deaths of the pilot and co-pilot increases the shock. Decision-making under such circumstances is extremely difficult. Such a situation requires a strong emphasis on the use of reasoning for making decisions and for reducing fear and panic.

Shock would be shown in the survivors by feelings of helplessness, loneliness, hopelessness, and fear. These feelings have brought about more fatalities than perhaps any other cause in survival situations. Certainly the state of shock means the movement of the survivors should be at a minimum, and that an attempt to calm them should be made.

Before taking off, a pilot has to file a flight plan which contains vital information such as the course, speed, estimated time of arrival, type of aircraft, and number of passengers. Search-and rescue operations begin shortly after the failure of a plane to appear at its destination at the estimated time of arrival.

The 20 miles to the nearest town is a long walk under even ideal conditions, particularly if one is not used to walking such distances. In this situation, the walk is even more difficult due to shock, snow, dress, and water barriers. It would mean almost certain death from freezing and exhaustion. At temperatures of minus 25 to minus 40, the loss of body heat through exertion is a very serious matter.

DE-BRIEF AND REVIEW:

Once the survivors have found ways to keep warm, their next task is to attract the attention of search planes. Thus, all the items the group has salvaged must be assessed for their value in signalling the group's whereabouts.

This survival simulation game is used in military training classrooms.

How to score

Each team should list its top 5 choices in order prior to seeing the answer sheet. To award points, look at the ranking numbers on this answer sheet. Award points to each team's top choices according to the numbers here. For example, the map would earn 12 points, while the steel wool would earn 2 points. Lowest score wins (and survives).

RANKINGS

1. Cigarette lighter (without fluid)

The gravest danger facing the group is exposure to cold. The greatest need is for a source of warmth and the second greatest need is for signalling devices. This makes building a fire the first order of business. Without matches, something is needed to produce sparks, and even without fluid, a cigarette lighter can do that.

2. Ball of steel wool

To make a fire, the survivors need a means of catching he sparks made by the cigarette lighter. This is the best substance for catching a spark and supporting a flame, even if the steel wool is a little wet.

3. Extra shirt and pants for each survivor

Besides adding warmth to the body, clothes can also be used for shelter, signalling, bedding, bandages, string (when unravelled), and fuel for the fire.

4. Can of Crisco shortening

This has many uses. A mirror-like signalling device can be made from the lid. After shining the lid with steel wool, it will reflect sunlight and generate 5 to 7 million candlepower. This is bright enough to be seen beyond the horizon. While this could be limited somewhat by the trees, a member of the group could climb a tree and use the mirrored lid to signal search planes. If they had no other means of signalling than this, they would have a better than 80% chance of being rescued within the first day. There are other uses for this item. It can be rubbed on exposed skin for protection against the cold. When melted into oil, the shortening is helpful as fuel. When soaked into a piece of cloth, melted shortening will act like a candle. The empty can is useful in melting snow for drinking water. It is much safer to drink warmed water than to eat snow, since warm water will help retain body heat. Water is important because dehydration will affect decision-making. The can is also useful as a cup.

5. 20 x 20 foot piece of canvas

The cold makes shelter necessary, and canvas would protect against wind and snow (canvas is used in making tents). Spread on a frame made of trees, it could be used as a tent or a wind screen. It might also be used as a ground cover to keep the survivors dry. It's shape, when contrasted with the surrounding terrain, makes it a signalling device.

DE-BRIEF AND REVIEW:

---

6. Small axe

Survivors need a constant supply of wood in order to maintain the fire. The axe could be used for this as well as for clearing a sheltered campsite, cutting tree branches for ground insulation, and constructing a frame for the canvas tent.

7. Family size chocolate bars (one per person)

Chocolate will provide some food energy. Since it contains mostly carbohydrates, it supplies the energy without making digestive demands on the body.

8. Newspapers (one per person)

These are useful in starting a fire. They can also be used as insulation under clothing when rolled up and placed around a person's arms and legs. A newspaper can also be used as a verbal signalling device when rolled up in a megaphone-shape. It could also provide reading material for recreation.

9. Loaded .45-caliber pistol

The pistol provides a sound-signalling device. (The international distress signal is 3 shots fired in rapid succession). There have been numerous cases of survivors going undetected because they were too weak to make a loud enough noise to attract attention. The butt of the pistol could be used as a hammer, and the powder from the shells will assist in fire building. By placing a small bit of cloth in a cartridge emptied of its bullet, one can start a fire by firing the gun at dry wood on the ground. The pistol also has some serious disadvantages. Anger, frustration, impatience, irritability, and lapses of rationality may increase as the group awaits rescue. The availability of a lethal weapon is a danger to the group under these conditions. Although a pistol could be used in hunting, it would take an expert marksman to kill an animal with it. Then the animal would have to be transported to the crash site, which could prove difficult to impossible depending on its size.

10. Quart of 100 proof whiskey

The only uses of whiskey are as an aid in fire building and as a fuel for a torch (made by soaking a piece of clothing in the whiskey and attaching it to a tree branch). The empty bottle could be used for storing water. The danger of whiskey is that someone might drink it, thinking it would bring warmth. Alcohol takes on the temperature it is exposed to, and a drink of minus 30 degrees Fahrenheit whiskey would freeze a person's oesophagus and stomach. Alcohol also dilates the blood vessels in the skin, resulting in chilled blood being carried back to the heart, resulting in a rapid loss of body heat. Thus, a drunk person is more likely to get hypothermia than a sober person is.

11. Compass

Because a compass might encourage someone to try to walk to the nearest town, it is a dangerous item. It's only redeeming feature is that it could be used as a reflector of sunlight (due to its glass top).

12. Sectional air map made of plastic

This is also among the least desirable of the items because it will encourage individuals to try to walk to the nearest town. It's only useful feature is as a ground cover to keep someone dry.

TERRY'S MOTEL

OBJECTIVE:

To help groups identify what can be done to avoid issues happening or being repeated in the future. Helps people recognise that rather than apportioning blame, putting plans in place to avoid the same mistakes happening again can be more helpful.

MATERIAL REQUIRED:	TIME REQUIRED:
• A sheet for everyone with the story on it.	10 – 15 minutes
• A whiteboard to record groups responses	

INSTRUCTIONS:

Explain that the group must get into pairs or threes. You will read them a story (or hand out the story for them to read as a pair or threes.)

Once they have read through or listened to the story, they must decide who was responsible for the mess.

STORY: For Terry, it was the worst day he had ever had in the six years he and his wife Pauline had been managing the motel. She had been browbeating him for three months to get some builders in to close off some doors and open up others because, she said, it was just "impossible" to go on the way things were.

Terry couldn't really see the point or the problem, as everyone had managed quite well for many years. However, for the sake of peace and quiet, he had agreed. He had booked the builders to come last week, and of course, at the last moment they cancelled and said they could only come yesterday, which was his long-awaited fishing day. Pauline would have to organise them, which to his surprise, she had agreed to do. So off he went fishing, only to learn later of the ensuing fiasco. After he had gone, Pauline remembered it was her turn to lead off at the club competition, which she couldn't possibly miss, so she called in Jenny, the duty manager, to handle it, and left. Soon after, Jenny, who had been up half the night because the night porter hadn't turned up for work, headed for a room for a nap. She left a note for the receptionist to wake her as soon as the builders arrived.

Jenny, who was quite overwhelmed with work, and got herself into a tizz, forgot about sleeping in the room, went outside and promptly fell asleep under a tree. When the workers arrived, Leanne the receptionist couldn't find Jenny, but remembered seeing Bob, the barman talking to Terry about door changes or something and sent the workers off to talk with him.

Bob, always eager to please, took them under his friendly wing on a tour of the motel, and gave them clear instructions about what Terry had said he wanted to be changed. He got it completely wrong.

Your task:

In pairs, decide which character is most responsible for the mess.

DE-BRIEF AND REVIEW:

- Record their responses on a whiteboard if you like. Ask them why they made their choice.

- Explain that in reality, mess-ups happen and in fairness, everyone could have done something to avoid it.

- Have the group share what each person could have done to help avoid the mess

- Explain that it is more important to look for ways to avoid messes in the future than to apportion blame – especially when lots of things could have contributed.

Training Support Team

THE JACKET

OBJECTIVE:

To illustrate the difference between one way and two way communication. This also highlights areas such as how much jargon is used and how simple tasks can become complicated when no visual clues are available (such as over the telephone).

MATERIAL REQUIRED:	TIME REQUIRED:
Two volunteers	15 - 20 minutes
One jacket	

INSTRUCTIONS:

Ask for two volunteers from the group

When you have two people, ask one to stay in the room while you take the other person outside. Explain to the person outside that this is an activity in communication and there are two parts to it. They will be standing back to back and the person in the room will be telling them how to put their jacket on, at this stage they are not allowed to ask questions, respond or acknowledge the instructions, they just do it.

Tell the person that to drive the point home you want them to do what they are told BUT to do it wrong; for example when told to pick the jacket up (assumption they will pick it up the right way), they do so, but upside down. When told to put their arm in a sleeve (assumption they know what a sleeve is) they put their hand in a pocket etc.

Return back to the room and ask the two people to stand back to back at the front of the room.

Explain to the group that person A (using their name) is an alien from another planet and has just come to Earth for a holiday! The problem is that Earth is a lot colder than their planet and therefore person B's (using their name) job is to simply tell them how to put on the jacket before they freeze.

Person A can understand and speak English but they are not allowed to ask questions or answer questions they simply must do as they are told.

At NO time must they turn around to see what is happening

Then start in their own time to begin and watch what happens.

This carries on until the person giving the instructions thinks the other person has the jacket on correctly. (you may need to prompt them such as "yes they have done that, do you think they have it on now?")

Ask them to turn around and face each other and see the outcome of their instructions. (This should be hilarious!)

Now ask them to turn back around, (putting the jacket back on the floor again) and complete the exercise again but this time both parties can ask questions, clarify points, confirm instructions. For example Person A "I want you to pick up the jacket by the collar"

Person B putting on the jacket replies with "what is a collar?" etc.

This continues until they are sure they have it right, then ask them to turn around and see the results. This time it should be correct.

What will happen:

The person giving the instructions will jump to a number of assumptions such as how easy it is to put on a jacket, they will understand or know what the jargon means such as collar, sleeves, buttons, zips etc.

The second time two way communication occurs and these statements get clarified until the end result is the jacket being put on correctly.

DE-BRIEF AND REVIEW:

Ask person A:

- "What was so hard about telling someone to put a jacket on?
- "Which was more successful first or second? What was different?
- How much easier was it to put on the jacket when you could ask questions and get clarification on points you didn't understand?
- What jargon was used? Sleeves, collar, cuffs, etc.

Explain to the group how many times have we assumed the customer understands what we are saying over the telephone when we have no visual clues?

What jargon do we use on a daily basis because we are familiar with that could be confusing the customer? How can we say this in a different way so the customer will understand?

What happens when we make assumptions about the level of knowledge a customer has when doing business with us? What are some the issues this can / has caused in the past?

TOO MUCH TOOTHPASTE

OBJECTIVE:

To illustrate what happens if we try to cram in too much of the same thing at once. It shows the pointlessness of overdoing the same activity and why we get more value when doing the same thing over different periods of time rather than all at once. Consider exercise, revision, reading etc

MATERIAL REQUIRED:	TIME REQUIRED:
• Toothbrush	5 minutes
• Tube of toothpaste	
• Willing volunteer	

INSTRUCTIONS:

Ask which of the group may have forgotten to brush their teeth that morning. In most cases, no-one will own up but you may get someone who does. You could ask if someone fancied a second brushing or someone who wish they'd spent a bit more time brushing their teeth. In any case, ask someone to volunteer to come forward for the opportunity to get cleaner teeth.

With the volunteer. Ask them to hold the tooth brush carefully (you may like to put a paper towel underneath) then proceed to empty the whole toothpaste tube onto the brush.

Suggest to the person that they could save time by brushing their teeth now for a whole month in advance.

Ask the group what they think. Of course it's not effective to brush your teeth with a whole tube of toothpaste for the month. It makes little difference for one day but a huge difference if you skip the rest of the month.

DE-BRIEF AND REVIEW:

ASK THEM

- Why would that not work effectively?
- What else could we apply that principle to for our group?

TOOTHPASTE WORDS

OBJECTIVE:

To illustrate that sometimes we cannot take back negative words we have said. This is useful when talking about communication, customer interaction, bullying etc.

MATERIAL REQUIRED:	TIME REQUIRED:
Tube of toothpaste and a bowl	5 minutes

INSTRUCTIONS:

Ask for a volunteer to come to the front of the group. Give them to the toothpaste tube and the bowl. Ask them to squeeze the toothpaste into the bowl.

When they have squeezed it all out, tell them to put the toothpaste back in the tube. After they try or protest, tell them that they must do it and push them to try harder.

When the volunteer is sure they can't put the toothpaste back, thank them and ask them to return to their seat.

DE-BRIEF AND REVIEW:

Explain to the group that the toothpaste is like negative, rude or unkind comments. Once they are out, they are so difficult – sometimes impossible to put back. You could then lead into a further discussion about communication relative to the group and the session.

VALUES COMPASS

OBJECTIVE:

To reinforce the company values and explore the benefits of having shared values as a group.

MATERIAL REQUIRED:	TIME REQUIRED:
• 2 flip charts • markers • 2 blindfolds	20 - 30 minutes

INSTRUCTIONS:

Prepare the flip charts by drawing a simple spiral path on each of them. The path should have vertical and horizontal straight lines. Draw the following path on the first flip chart:

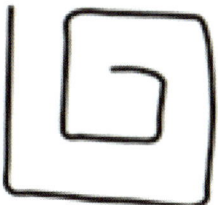

Draw the following path on the second flip chart:

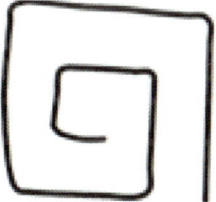

FLOW

1. Introduce the company values and discuss the importance of these values.

2. Divide the participants into two groups. Ask each group to create a compass using the five values (most companies have five values) writing each value randomly into one of the boxes in a compass figure (as shown below) to create their compass.

3. Ask each team to nominate a member to be blindfolded. Ask this member to memorize the values compass before they are blindfolded. Inform the blindfolded people that they will have to trace the line from the beginning to the end. They will be guided by their teammates who will be shouting the values to direct them

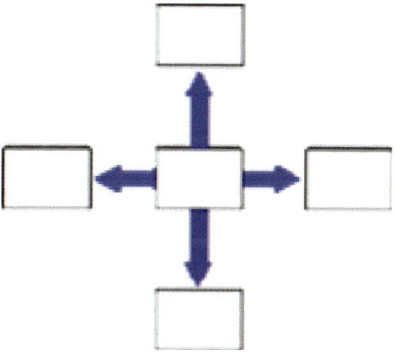

4. Explain the constraints. Team members cannot touch the blindfolded person. They may not use words that refer to directions (such as North, East, South, West, up, down, left, or right).

1. Start the activity by placing the index finger of the blindfolded participants at the beginning location. Ask the teammates to give directions by using only the values they wrote on the compass figure. The blindfolded participant should move their finger along the line. If their finger goes off the line, they have to return to the beginning and start all over again.

2. Give useful tips. Point out that the value associated with the middle position of the compass is the equivalent of "Stop". Suggest to the blindfolded person that they move their finger slowly and be ready to stop whenever her teammates yell out the appropriate value.

3. When one of the blindfolded participants reaches the ending location inside the matrix, stop the activity. Congratulate the winning contestant and their team of advisors.

DE-BRIEF AND REVIEW:

ASK THEM

- You did not specify a goal for the path tracing activity. The two groups may focus on different outcomes: one may focus on quality while the other may focus on speed. What is the consequence of these different goals? Where do we find such alternative goals in our company?

- In some groups, participants may enthusiastically shout out values directions, while in other groups, participants may consider the activity to be trivial and leave one person to shout out navigation suggestions for the blindfolded person. What makes participants have different preferences and values?

- What roles evolved in the two groups? What were similar and what were different?

- If we define values as shared set of principles, how do we all live the values in our company?

Training Support Team

WALK THE BEAM

OBJECTIVE:

To illustrate how motivation is a changeable element dependent upon the circumstances.

MATERIAL REQUIRED:	TIME REQUIRED:
None	10 minutes

INSTRUCTIONS:

Explain to the group that you have a big solid steel beam on the back of a truck and it is going to be placed directly on the road outside your house. Show the group the width and depth of this beam.

Re-iterate to the group that this beam (describe the width and depth again) will be laid on the ground in front of their house.

Ask the group "If I give you $100.00 would you walk across the length of the beam"

Go around the group and get their responses – clarify if the group ask questions – DO NOT ask WHY if someone says "NO" at this point.

Explain to the group that this time the beam (describe the measurements again) will be balanced between (pick two tall land marks in your location or two landmarks or tall buildings people will know)

Explain that the weather is windy and wet and the beam will be slippery and they have NO safety harness or ropes

Ask the group "If I give you $100.00 would you walk across the beam"

Go around the group – same as above.

This time get the group to visualise (close their eyes to get a clear picture) of someone or something they love dearly. Give them time to get this picture clear in their head.

Go over the scenario again with the beam balanced between two tall buildings.

Tell the group that you are standing at one end of the beam holding the someone or something they love dearly by the wrist and will let them go unless they get across the beam

Tell the group that "If you do not come across the beam I will let this someone or something go"

Ask the group – would you do it? Would get across the beam?

As above go around the room and get responses.

DE-BRIEF AND REVIEW:

Explain that motivation can be positive and dangerous – however we need to know what motivates us before we can achieve our full potential.

We also need to understand how fast we can change our reason for wanting to complete something if we have the right motivation to do so.

WHO IS HAPPIER?

OBJECTIVE:

To illustrate the reality that we all have a perspective from which we see things. It helps to see things from someone else perspective to get an overall view.

MATERIAL REQUIRED:	TIME REQUIRED:
Sheet containing the image shown in the instructions	10 minutes

INSTRUCTIONS:

Show the group a copy of the image that appears below and ask them to determine who looks happier.

The responses from the group are likely to be as follows:

If you are right handed, you probably think the character on the right is happier.

If you are left-handed, the happier one is likely to be the one on the left.

This test was devised by the psychologist Julian Jaynes to show how our perception is affected by our left-right lateralisation of our brains.

About 90% of right handed persons consider the right face to be more friendly, about 60% of the left handed persons say the left face.

DE-BRIEF AND REVIEW:

ASK THEM

- What can perspective do in our roles – good and bad?
- How can we use this in our roles?

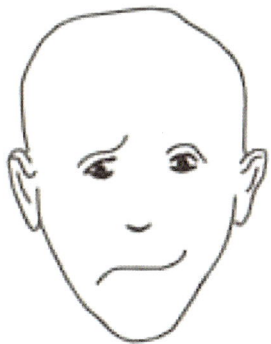 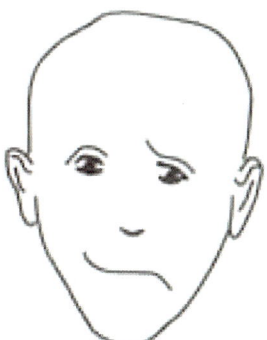

WHO OWNS THE ZEBRA?

OBJECTIVE:

This is a problem solving activity. It will provide an opportunity for groups to logically work through some provided information to work out the required solution. As teams need to work together, it's a great team building activity also.

MATERIAL REQUIRED:	TIME REQUIRED:
Information sheets per group	20 – 30 minutes

INSTRUCTIONS:

Divide the wider group into at least two groups. Group sizes shouldn't be too large so it allows for everyone to participate. Groups of 2-4 would be ideal.

Explain to the group that you will be giving them some instructions to help solve a problem that involves logic.

They will get some information that consists of facts about some houses in a street and they must work out 'who owns the zebra?' and 'who drinks the water?'

These two answers can be worked out by using the provided information to establish a solution to all the information.

The participant's task is to resolve the puzzle as quickly as possible.

Here is the information to provide on a sheet to each group:

Use your powers of deduction to answer the questions at the bottom of this page. The clues supplied give you all the information you require to solve the puzzle and you only need to use logic to do so.

The list below gives you information about a little street. There are five houses in a row in this little street. Each one of the houses has a different door colour and behind each of these doors lives a person of a different nationality. Every one of these people has a different pet, enjoys a different drink and works in a different profession.

1. The Englishwoman lives in the red house.
2. The Spaniard owns a dog.
3. Coffee is drunk in the greenhouse
4. The Ukrainian drinks tea.
5. The green house is immediately to the right of the Ivory house.
6. The engineer owns the snail.
7. The diplomat lives in the yellow house.
8. Milk is drunk in the middle house.
9. The Norwegian lives in the first house on the left.
10. The doctor lives next to the owner of the fox.
11. The diplomat lives next to the owner of the horse.
12. The teacher drinks orange juice.
13. The carpenter is Japanese.
14. The Norwegian lives next to the blue house.

Question: Who owns the zebra? And Who drinks the water?

DE-BRIEF AND REVIEW:

Firstly, here is the solution:

To help find the solution you can put the information in order that has been provided. Put the houses in order so you have an easier to track each person.

The Englishwoman lives in the red house, so we can record that on a simple list as below. The Spaniard owns a dog, so again we can add that information to our list too.

If we follow this route, we can slowly build a complete list of information which gives us this information:

House	1	2	3	4	5
Door	Yellow	Blue	Red	Ivory	Green
Nationality	Norwegian	Ukrainian	Englishman	Spaniard	Japanese
Drink	Water	Tea	Milk	Orange	Coffee
Job	Diplomat	Doctor	Engineer	Teacher	Carpenter
Pet	Fox	Horse	Snail	Dog	Zebra

As a result, we can deduce the following:

The Japanese person owns the zebra and the water is drunk by the Norwegian.

Discuss how the participants approached the problem, what worked, what didn't work and what they might do differently next time. Was there a strategy? What was it? Did it work?

If one person or group of people found the task easier than others, discuss why this might be and what lessons could be learned.

TRAINING REVIEW ACTIVITIES

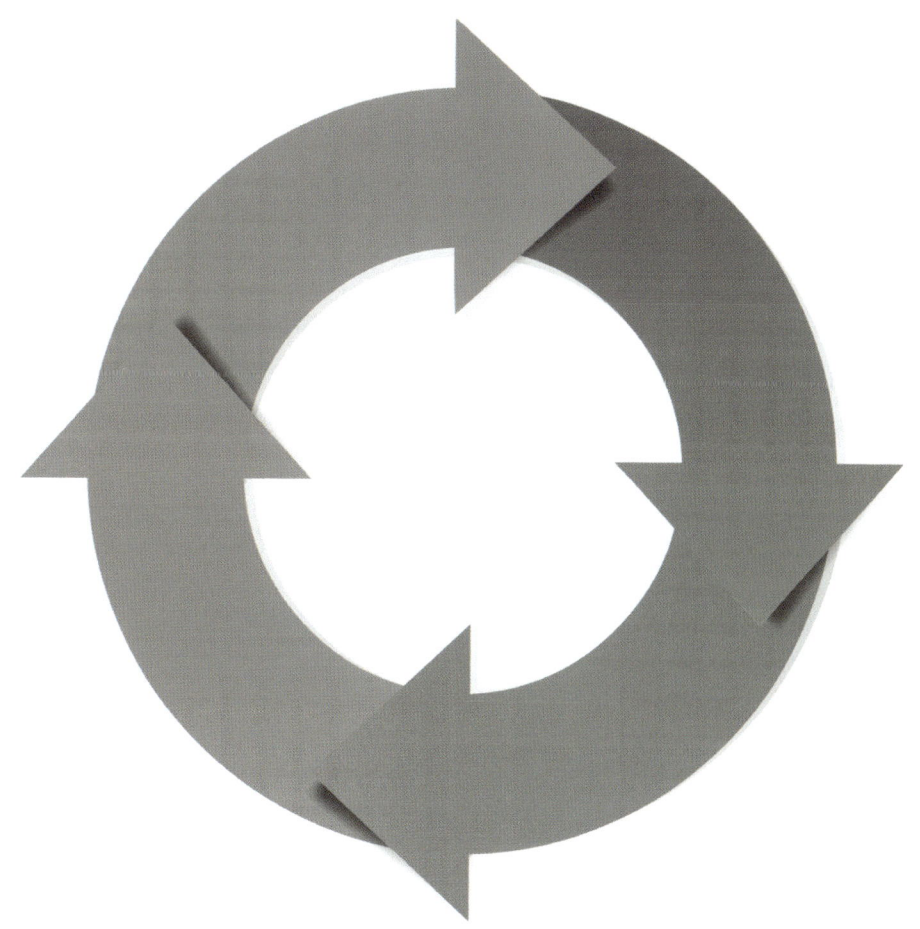

ACRONYM BUBBLE

OBJECTIVE:

This activity is useful to help people to remember things from the session. It also helps them to get creative and solidify learning.

MATERIAL REQUIRED:	TIME REQUIRED:
None	10 - 15 minutes

INSTRUCTIONS:

Pick a word based on the session you have been running or a product or a key learning point or even something you've made up.

Write the word on a flipchart and surround it with the statement… If… {Your Word} …were an acronym, what would it stand for?

Ask participants to come up with as many great acronyms as they can based on the word suggested.

FOR EXAMPLE:

If… Hat …was the acronym, what could it stand for?

Head Always Topped

Happy And Trimmed

Habitually Always Trapped

DE-BRIEF AND REVIEW:

Get them to record any they think will help them recall the key topic, product or whatever you chose.

APPS ACTIVITY

OBJECTIVE:

To help the group solidify ideas and thinking from some of the principles covered off in training. Ideal for a day two review of day one or a recap moment.

MATERIAL REQUIRED:	TIME REQUIRED:
A3 sheet prepared with APPS	20 - 30 minutes

INSTRUCTIONS:

Prepare an A3 sheet for each group that has some popular APP symbols and space for them to write in. Alternatively just give them a blank sheet of flipchart paper and suggest a layout. For example, the following could be used with an explanation of each:

- # - create one or two hashtags that sum up our learnings from day one
- Spotify – share a song title that sums up a learning point
- Snapchat / Instagram – draw a picture that encapsulates a learning point
- Google – what question did we answer from the session?
- APPly – What will you do to apply the learning?

Give the team a time limit – 10 – 15 minutes to come up with suitable responses that they will then share back with the group.

Have them share back with the group and then pin them up on the wall as a reminder.

DE-BRIEF AND REVIEW:

ASK THEM

- What will they do to remember what they have learned
- How will they apply the learnings?

GROUP REVIEW

OBJECTIVE:

To remind each other of the key learning points from a session.

MATERIAL REQUIRED:	TIME REQUIRED:
Koosh Ball or similar	5 - 10 MINUTES

INSTRUCTIONS:

Have everybody stand up in the group. Form a circle it helps.

Hold up a Koosh ball and explain that we will all have an opportunity to share something about the session. Explain that someone will start off with the Koosh ball and share something from the session. You can vary it up a bit but consider the following phrases to choose from:

"Share something you learned from the session"

"Tell the group one thing you're going to leave behind as a result of the session"

"Share one thing you will take away from the session"

Then that person throws the Koosh ball to someone else in the group. Explain that we would like to hear from everyone in the group so throw it to someone who hasn't shared something yet.

DE-BRIEF AND REVIEW:

Thank the group and congratulate them on what they've learned and are willing to do.

PERFORMANCE TIME

OBJECTIVE:

To help the group solidify learnings from the session, induction, product knowledge or any learnings you want them to remember better. This activity is a great energizer and requires the group to be creative and step outside their comfort zone.

MATERIAL REQUIRED:	TIME REQUIRED:
None	10 – 20 minutes

INSTRUCTIONS:

Divide the wider group into smaller groups of 3-6 people. Explain that it's now time for a performance. In their groups they are to come up with either:

- A song
- A rap
- An advert
- A dramatization
- A skit
- Whatever they choose….

That summarises the key learnings from the day, the induction programme, their sales conference or whatever is the most appropriate setting.

Give them 5-10 minutes to prepare their performance, after which they will present back to the wider group!

DE-BRIEF AND REVIEW:

ASK THEM

- How could this work for induction programmes?
- How else could they use this?

Training Support Team

PLANE QUESTIONS

OBJECTIVE:

To help the group review what the session is about or to help them review current products or services. An excellent energizer or activity to use after lunch or on day two of a session.

MATERIAL REQUIRED:	TIME REQUIRED:
A piece of A4 paper for each person	10 – 15 minutes

INSTRUCTIONS:

Ask participants to write a question relating to the session that they are currently involved in or about a product or service the business offers in the middle of a sheet of A4 paper.

Then ask the group to make a paper aeroplane out of the sheets of paper with the question on. If they cannot make aeroplanes, ask them to make a ball out of the paper.

When everyone is ready, divide them into to two different lines facing each other and at opposite sides of the room.

Then ask them to throw their planes across the room at each other. When a plane lands near them, they must throw it back to the line of people on the other side of the room.

After one minute, stop the throwing and ask each participant to pick up the paper that is closest to them, open up the paper and one by one have the participants read and then answer the question on the paper.

DE-BRIEF AND REVIEW:

Congratulate the group on their plan making skills, throwing and ability to answer the questions. Consider asking if anyone would like to spend more time on any of the topics that came up.

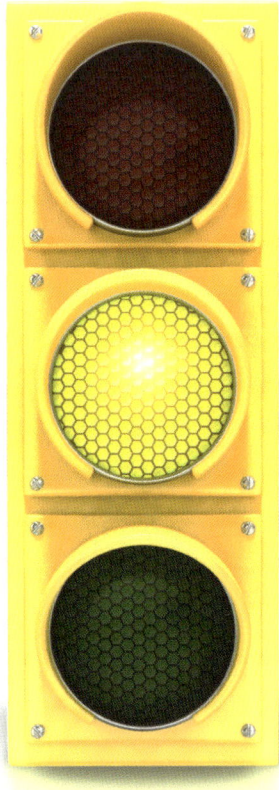

STOP, START, CONTINUE

OBJECTIVE:

A useful activity to use at the end of a session. It helps people focus on the application of what has been covered and discussed. It will also provide a good catalyst for discussion for a participant and their manager when they return to the workplace.

MATERIAL REQUIRED:	TIME REQUIRED:
Pen and paper for each participant	5 minutes

INSTRUCTIONS:

As a result of what has been discussed in the session, ask the participants to consider the following:

- What are two things you will start doing as a result of your experience in the session today?
- What are two things you will stop doing?
- What are two things you will continue to do?

You could suggest one thing for each part if you feel two is too many.

DE-BRIEF AND REVIEW:

Invite the group to share some of their commitments

STORIES

We thought we would also give you some of our most favoured and used stories that we use through our training to help drive home an important point while giving the group a chance to sit back relax and enjoy a short break, enjoy.

THE BEDBUG LETTER

OBJECTIVE:

To illustrate the care we need to take when providing Customer Service and managing customer complaints

MATERIAL REQUIRED:	TIME REQUIRED:
None	5 minutes (Approximately)

STORY:

Explain to the group that this is based on a real story in the States

There was a travelling salesman who travelled across the States

He used the sleeper trains as his means of transport. While on a trip he noticed that there were bedbugs and lice in his bed. As you can imagine he was not impressed. He wrote to the train company and complained about his experience.

The travelling salesman received a letter back from the train company and the response read:

Dear Sir,

Thank you so much for informing us of your unfortunate experience. I just want to let you know what actions we have taken;

1) Decommissioned the carriage you were in

2) All of the furniture and bedding has been taken out and destroyed.

3) The carriage has been completely disinfected

4) The cleaning crew have been fired

5) The guard in charge of the carriage has been severely reprimanded

6) A letter has been sent to all the crew that this is not to happen in the future

Once again thank you so much for bringing this to our attention. We look forward to your continued service.

The salesman was very impressed and was putting the letter back in the envelope when he noticed a post it note stuck on the back of the letter. The post it note read

"Send this Jerk the Bed Bug Letter"

As a result he took the company to court and won millions.

You can purchase this book online - it is called "Send this jerk the bed bug story"

DE-BRIEF AND REVIEW:

ASK THEM

- How did you feel when you heard about what the company had done as a result of his complaint? Impressed, amazed?

- How did that change when you realised they knew about the issue and this was a standard letter?

- How can you ensure you make your customers feel like you first did when they complain to you and not how you felt afterwards like a standard response?

CARROTS, EGGS AND COFFEE: OVERCOMING ADVERSITY

OBJECTIVE:

To illustrate how different people react to pressure or difficult situations.

MATERIAL REQUIRED:	TIME REQUIRED:
None	5 minutes (Approximately)

STORY:

A daughter complained to her father about her life and how things were so hard for her. She did not how she was going to make it and wanted to give up. She was tired of fighting and struggling. It seemed as one problem was solved a new one arose.

Her father, a chef, took her to the kitchen. He filled three pots with water and placed each on a high fire. Soon the pots came to a boil. In one he placed carrots, in the second he placed eggs, and in the last he placed ground coffee beans. He let them sit and boil, without saying a word.

The daughter sucked her teeth and impatiently waited, wondering what he was doing. After about twenty minutes he turned off the burners. He fished the carrots out and placed them in a bowl. He pulled the eggs out and placed them in a bowl. Then he laded the coffee out and placed it in a mug.

Turning to her, he asked: "Darling, what do you see?"

"Carrots, eggs, and coffee," she replied.

He brought her closer and asked her to feel the carrots. She did and noted that they were soft. He then asked her to take an egg and break it. After pulling off the shell, she observed the hard-boiled egg. Finally, he asked her to sip the coffee. She smiled as she tasted its rich aroma.

She humbly asked. "What does it mean?"

He explained that each of them had faced the same adversity, boiling water, but each reacted differently. The carrot went in strong, hard, and unrelenting. But after being subjected to the boiling water, it softened and became weak.

The egg had been fragile. Its thin outer shell had protected its liquid interior. But after sitting through the boiling water, its inside became hardened.

The ground coffee beans were unique however. After they were in the boiling water, they had changed the water.

"Which are you?" he asked his daughter, "When adversity knocks on your door, how do you respond? Are you a carrot, an egg, or a coffee bean?"

If you are like the bean, when things are at their worst, you get better and make things better around you.

How do you handle adversity? Are you a carrot, an egg, or a coffee bean?

DE-BRIEF AND REVIEW:

ASK THEM

- How about YOU? Are you the carrot, that seems hard, but with pain and adversity do you wilt and become soft and lose your strength?

- Are you the egg, which starts off with a malleable heart? Were you a fluid spirit, but after a death, a breakup, a divorce, or a layoff have you become hardened and stiff? Your shell looks the same, but are you bitter and tough with a stiff spirit and heart?

- Or are you like the coffee bean? The bean changes the hot water, the thing that is bringing the pain, to its peak flavor when it reaches 100° C. When the water gets the hottest, it just tastes better.

SHIPS IN THE NIGHT

OBJECTIVE:

To illustrate the importance of focusing what you can change and not wasting your time on things you have no control over.

MATERIAL REQUIRED:	TIME REQUIRED:
None	5 minutes (Approximately)

STORY:

A story often told by Stephen Covey, the renowned author of The Seven Habits of Highly Effective People. The story goes something like this:

It was a dark and stormy night. A radar operator woke the ships captain to report a blip on the radar directly in their path, 20 miles ahead; a ship that refused to move.

"Tell it to move!" said the irritated captain.

'We did and refuses to' said the operator.

The captain, furious, rose from his bed and sent the message himself; 'Shift your course 20 degrees starboard'.

A message comes back 'YOU shift YOUR course 20 degrees starboard'.

'What presumption! Don't know they know who I am?' Let them know who I am!' Said the captain.

The signal goes out 'This is Captain Horatio Hornblower the 26th, commanding you to move 20 degrees to starboard at once'.

The signal returns 'THIS is seaman Carl Jones the THIRD commanding YOU to move 20 degrees to starboard at once'.

The captain is LIVID with rage "What presumption! Who are these people? I mean, we are a battleship! Let them know who we are." And the signal goes out

"This is the MIGHTY Missouri, flagship of the seventh fleet. You are directly in our path. Move at once or face the consequences!"

The signal returns…..

"This is a lighthouse your call!"

DE-BRIEF AND REVIEW:

ASK THEM

- Think about some things in your life you are trying to change that you have no chance of changing?
- What can you focus on that you can change?

EYE OPENER

OBJECTIVE:

To illustrate the fact that people remember how we make them feel. Motivation / attitude

MATERIAL REQUIRED:	TIME REQUIRED:
None	5 minutes (Approximately)

STORY:

Read these first questions out quickly

Try this quiz:

1) Name the 5 wealthiest people in the world
2) Name the last 5 Miss World competition winners
3) Name 5 people who have won the Noble or Pulitzer prize
4) Name the last 5 Academy award winners for best actor / best actress

How did you do?

The point is none of us remember the headliners of yesterday. These are no second rate achievers, they are the best in their fields. But the applause dies, the awards tarnish and achievements are forgotten.

Here's another quiz, see how you do on this one but do this one in your head only.

1) List a few teachers who helped you through school
2) Name a few heroes/heroines who have inspired you
3) Name three friends who helped you through a difficult time
4) Name 5 people who have taught you something worthwhile
5) Think of a few people who have made you feel special
6) Think of some people you like spending time with

Was that easier?

DE-BRIEF AND REVIEW:

ASK THEM

- The people who make a difference in your life are not the ones with the most money, credentials or awards but the people who care.
- How do you think you make other people feel?

HOW TO STOP GOSSIP

OBJECTIVE:

To illustrate the importance of true and correct information and to avoid idle and damaging gossip.

MATERIAL REQUIRED:	TIME REQUIRED:
None	5 minutes (Approximately)

STORY:

Keep this philosophy in mind the next time you either hear or are about to repeat a rumour:

In ancient Greece (469 - 399 BC), Socrates was widely lauded for his wisdom. One day the great philosopher came upon an acquaintance who ran up to him excitedly and said,

"Socrates, do you know what I just heard about one of your students?"

"Wait a moment," Socrates replied. "Before you tell me I'd like you to pass a little test. It's called the Triple Filter Test."

"Triple filter?"

"That's right," Socrates continued. "Before you talk to me about my student let's take a moment to filter what you're going to say. The first filter is truth. Have you made absolutely sure that what you are about to tell me is true?"

"No," the man said, "actually I just heard about it."

"All right," said Socrates. "So you don't really know if it's true or not.

Now let's try the second filter, the filter of Goodness. Is what you are about to tell me about my student something good?"

"No, on the contrary ..."

"So," Socrates continued, "you want to tell me something bad about him, even though you're not certain it's true?"

The man shrugged, a little embarrassed. Socrates continued." You may still pass the test though, because there is a third filter - the filter of Usefulness. Is what you want to tell me about my student going to be useful to me?"

"No, not really ..."

"Well," concluded Socrates, "if what you want to tell me is neither true nor good nor even useful, why tell it to me at all?"

The man was defeated and ashamed.

DE-BRIEF AND REVIEW:

ASK THEM

- Have you ever repeated / gossiped without checking the facts?
- What difference would it make if you followed these three points when hearing or repeating information?

MEXICAN FISHING VILLAGE

OBJECTIVE:

To illustrate the power of knowing where you are in your life and where you want to be. Motivation / Attitude / Planning

MATERIAL REQUIRED:	TIME REQUIRED:
None	5 minutes (Approximately)

STORY:

A boat docked in a tiny Mexican village. An American tourist complimented the Mexican fisherman on the quality of his fish and asked how long it took him to catch them.

"Not very long," answered the Mexican.

"But then, why didn't you stay out longer and catch more?" asked the American.

The Mexican explained that his small catch was sufficient to meet his needs and those of his family.

The American asked, "But what do you do with the rest of your time?"

"I sleep late, fish a little, play with my children, and take a siesta with my wife. In the evenings, I go into the village to see my friends, play the guitar, and sing a few songs... I have a full life."

The American interrupted, "I have an MBA from Harvard, and I can help you! You should start by fishing longer every day. You can then sell the extra fish you catch. With the extra revenue, you can buy a bigger boat."

"And after that?" asked the Mexican.

"With the extra money the larger boat will bring, you can buy a second one and a third one and so on until you have an entire fleet of trawlers. Instead of selling your fish to a middleman, you can then negotiate directly with the processing plants and maybe even open your own plant. You can then leave this little village and move to Mexico City, Los Angeles, or even New York City! From there you can direct your huge new enterprise."

"How long would that take?" asked the Mexican.

"Twenty, perhaps twenty-five years," replied the American.

"And after that?"

"Afterwards? Well my Friend, That's when it gets really interesting," answered the American, laughing. "When your business gets really big, you can start selling stocks and make millions!"

"Millions? Really? And after that?" said the Mexican.

"After that you'll be able to retire, live in a tiny village near the coast, sleep late, play with your children, catch a few fish, take a siesta with your wife and spend your evenings doing what you like and enjoying your friends."

DE-BRIEF AND REVIEW:

ASK THEM

- Are you happy with your current position?
- If not do you know where you want to end up?
- Do you have a plan to get there?

THE TOMATO COMPANY

OBJECTIVE:

To illustrate the fact that you shouldn't let things hold you back or let other people tell you whats important for you. Motivation / Attitude

MATERIAL REQUIRED:	TIME REQUIRED:
None	5 minutes (Approximately)

STORY:

An unemployed man is desperate to support his family of a wife and three kids. He applies for a janitor's job at a large firm and easily passes an aptitude test.

The human resources manager tells him, "You will be hired at minimum wage of $5.15 an hour. Let me have your e-mail address so that we can get you in the loop. Our system will automatically e-mail you all the forms and advise you when to start and where to report on your first day."

Taken back, the man protests that he is poor and has neither a computer nor an e-mail address. To this the manager replies, "You must understand that to a company like ours that means that you virtually do not exist. Without an e-mail address you can hardly expect to be employed by a high-tech firm. Good day."

Stunned, the man leaves. Not knowing where to turn and having $10 in his wallet, he walks past a farmers' market and sees a stand selling 25lb crates of beautiful red tomatoes. He buys a crate, carries it to a busy corner and displays the tomatoes. In less than 2 hours he sells all the tomatoes and makes 100% profit. Repeating the process several times more that day, he ends up with almost $100 and arrives home that night with several bags of groceries for his family.

During the night he decides to repeat the tomato business the next day. By the end of the week he is getting up early every day and working into the night. He multiplies his profits quickly. Early in the second week he acquires a cart to transport several boxes of tomatoes at a time, but before a month is up he sells the cart to buy a broken-down pickup truck.

At the end of a year he owns three old trucks. His two sons have left their neighborhood gangs to help him with the tomato business, his wife is buying the tomatoes, and his daughter is taking night courses at the community college so she can keep books for him.

By the end of the second year he has a dozen very nice used trucks and employs fifteen previously unemployed people, all selling tomatoes. He continues to work hard.

Time passes and at the end of the fifth year he owns a fleet of nice trucks and a warehouse that his wife supervises, plus two tomato farms that the boys manage. The tomato company's payroll has put hundreds of homeless and jobless people to work. His daughter reports that the business grossed a million dollars.

Planning for the future, he decides to buy some life insurance. Consulting with an insurance adviser, he picks an insurance plan to fit his new circumstances. Then the adviser asks him for his e-mail address in order to send the final documents electronically.

When the man replies that he doesn't have time to mess with a computer and has no e-mail address, the insurance man is stunned, "What, you don't have e-mail? No computer? No Internet? Just think where you would be today if you'd had all of that five years ago!"

"Ha!" snorts the man. "If I'd had e-mail five years ago I would be sweeping floors at Microsoft and making $5.15 an hour."

DE-BRIEF AND REVIEW:

ASK THEM

- What do you believe is limiting you from what you want to achieve?
- What can you start to do to overcome these limitations?
- What difference will it make if you overcome your limitations?

TIME MANAGEMENT FUNNY STORY

OBJECTIVE:

To illustrate the importance of completing one task before you get on with another. Time management / Plannning.

MATERIAL REQUIRED:	TIME REQUIRED:
None	5 minutes (Approximately)

STORY:

I need to wash my car. As I start toward the garage, I notice that there is mail on the hall table. I decide to go through the mail before washing the car. I put my car keys down on the table, put the junk mail in the trash under the table, and notice that the trash can is full. So, I decide to put the bills back on the table to take out the trash first.

But then I say to myself, since I'm going to be near the mailbox when I take out the trash anyway, I might as well pay the bills first. I take my cheque book off the table, and see that there is only one cheque left. My extra cheques are in my desk in the study, so I go to my desk where I find a bottle of coke that I had been drinking. I'm about to look for my cheques, but first I need to push the coke aside so that I wouldn't accidentally knock it over. I notice that the coke is getting warm, so I decide that I should put it in the refrigerator to keep it cold. I head towards the kitchen with the coke.

A vase of flowers on the counter catches my eye - they needed to be watered. As I put the coke down on the counter, I notice my reading glasses which I've been searching for all morning. I decide I had better take them back to my desk, but first I must water the flowers. I put the glasses back down on the counter, fill a container with water when suddenly I spot the I V remote.

Someone had left it on the kitchen table. I realise that tonight, when we go to watch TV, we will be looking for the remote, but nobody will remember that it's on the kitchen table, so I decide to take it back to the TV room where it belongs, but first I must water the flowers.

I splash some water on the flowers, but most of it spills on the floor. So, I put the remote back down on the table, to get some towels to wipe up the spill. Then I head down the hall trying to remember why I'm going that way and what I was planning to do.

Now, it's the end of the day; the car isn't washed, the bills aren't paid, there is a warm bottle of coke sitting on the counter, the flowers aren't watered, there is still only one cheque in my cheque book, I can't find the remote, I can't find my glasses, and I don't remember what I did with the car keys.

I try to figure out why nothing got done today. I'm really baffled because I know I was busy all day long and now I'm really tired. I realize this is a serious problem, and I'll try to get some help for it, but first I'll check my e-mail.

DE-BRIEF AND REVIEW:

ASK THEM

- What are the benefits of better time management?
- What things can you start doing to improve your time management?

Training Support Team

THE COMFORT ZONE POEM

OBJECTIVE:

To illustrate the importance of stepping outside your comfort zone

MATERIAL REQUIRED:	TIME REQUIRED:
None	5 minutes (Approximately)

STORY:

I used to have a comfort zone where I knew I wouldn't fail.

The same four walls and busywork were really like a jail.

I longed so much to do the things I'd never done before,

But stayed inside my comfort zone and paced the same old floor.

I said it didn't matter that I wasn't doing much.

I said I didn't care for things like commission checks and such.

I claimed to be so busy with the things inside the zone,

But deep inside I longed for something special of my own.

I couldn't let my life go by just watching others win.

I held my breath; I stepped outside and let the change begin.

I took a step and with new strength I'd never felt before,

I kissed my comfort zone goodbye and closed and locked the door.

If you're in a comfort zone, afraid to venture out,

Remember that all winners were at one time filled with doubt.

A step or two and words of praise can make your dreams come true.

Reach for your future with a smile; Success is there for you!

DE-BRIEF AND REVIEW:

ASK THEM

- Why is it important to challenge your comfort zone?
- What difference do you think it will make if you push outside your comfort zone?
- What's one thing you can do today to make a start?

Index of Topics List

Topic categories and associated page numbers for quick selection of activities to meet a specific need:

Problem Solving

29, 31, 41, 55, 61, 69, 73, 101, 109, 111, 115, 123, 127, 129, 31, 133, 143, 151, 155, 163, 165, 171, 173, 183, 187, 193, 197, 211, 223.

Stress

175.

Team bonding

17, 21, 23, 25, 27, 33, 35, 37, 39, 41, 43, 45, 47, 49, 51, 65, 77, 79, 81, 83, 89, 95, 97, 119, 127, 135, 145, 151, 159, 163, 165, 167, 169, 179, 183, 191, 221, 223.

Team Building

17, 19, 21, 29, 31, 55, 61, 65, 67, 73, 75, 95, 101, 109, 113, 123, 127, 131, 143, 155, 163, 165, 167, 171, 183, 187, 191, 193, 205, 217, 221.

Time management

127, 137, 155, 163, 187, 201, 221.

Printed in Great Britain
by Amazon